SCHOLASTIC

2013 BOOK OF WORLD RECORDS

by Jenifer Corr Morse

A GEORGIAN BAY BOOK

SCHOLASTIC INC.

To Isabelle Nicole—May you always find wonder in the world.
—JCM

CREATED AND PRODUCED BY GEORGIAN BAY LLC
Copyright © 2012 by Georgian Bay LLC

All rights reserved. Published by Scholastic Inc., *Publishers since 1920*. SCHOLASTIC and associated logos are trademarks and/or registered trademarks of Scholastic Inc.

GEORGIAN BAY STAFF
Bruce S. Glassman, Executive Editor
Jenifer Corr Morse, Author
Amy Stirnkorb, Designer

ISBN 978-0-545-42517-9

10 9 8 7 6 5 4 3 2   12 13 14 15 16

Printed in the U.S.A.   40
First edition, November 2012

In most cases, the graphs in this book represent the top five record holders in each category. However, in some graphs, we have chosen to list well-known or common people, places, animals, or things that will help you better understand how extraordinary the record holder is. These may not be the top five in the category. Additionally, some graphs have fewer than five entries because so few people or objects reflect the necessary criteria.

Due to the publication date, the majority of statistics is current as of May 2012.

CONTENTS

SCIENCE &
TECHNOLOGY
records

video games ○ internet ○ technology
vehicles ○ structures ○ travel
transportation ○ environment

THE WRITE STUFF

Wikipedia hosts more than 17 million articles that were written by about 91,000 authors and contributors. And it keeps getting bigger—the number of articles grew 21 percent between 2010 and 2011.

WIKIPEDIA
The Free Encyclopedia

TEXTING TAKEOVER

The average cell phone user sends 41.5 texts each day, which equals 15,147 texts each year. Almost three-quarters of all mobile phone users text, and about 31 percent actually prefer texting to calling.

CUT TO VIDEO

People spend about 2.9 billion hours on YouTube each month, which is roughly the same as 326,294 years. An average of 490 million unique users log on each month, generating about 92 billion page views during each 30-day period.

OUT OF THIS WORLD

On January 22, 2010, NASA astronaut T.J. Creamer sent the first unassisted off-Earth tweet—"Hello Twitterverse! We r now LIVE tweeting from the International Space Station—the 1st live tweet from Space! :) More soon, send your ?s."

THAT CALLS FOR APP-LAUSE

About 14 billion apps have been downloaded since the Apple store opened in July 2008, and the iPad accounts for about 10 percent of them. The average iPad user has downloaded more than 60 apps, and the top three paid apps are Pandora, Google mobile, and Movies by Flixter.

Fast Friends

Google+ was the fastest social network site to reach 10 million users—a feat it accomplished in just 16 days. Twitter took 780 days to register this many users, while Facebook took 852 days. Google+ currently has 25 million users worldwide.

Just Face It

There are more than 30 billion items shared on Facebook each month. One out of every nine people in the world accesses the site. If Facebook users formed a country, it would be the world's third-largest nation.

bestselling family video game

POKÉMON BLACK AND WHITE

Nintendo's Pokémon: Black and White was the top-seller of 2011 with more than 8.5 million games sold. The game debuted in Japan in late 2010, and then in North America in March 2011. Black and White is set in the fictional Unova, and gamers become young Pokémon trainers who collect animals to compete against one another. There are more than 150 new Pokémon in the Black and White versions. Although the Black and the White versions are separate titles, they have the same plot, and Pokémon need to be traded between the two versions to collect them all.

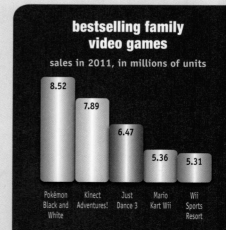

bestselling family video games

sales in 2011, in millions of units

Pokémon Black and White	Kinect Adventures!	Just Dance 3	Mario Kart Wii	Wii Sports Resort
8.52	7.89	6.47	5.36	5.31

WII

Since it was first released in November 2006, the Nintendo Wii has sold more than 95 million consoles throughout the world. The system is controlled by wireless remotes that mirror the users' body movements by relaying them to a sensor on the television. The Wii can connect to the Internet, and also to other Wii consoles. The console's name—pronounced "we"—means that everyone can play. Some of the more than 1,200 games available include Wii Sports, Mario Kart Wii, Wii Fit, Just Dance, Guitar Hero, and The Legend of Zelda.

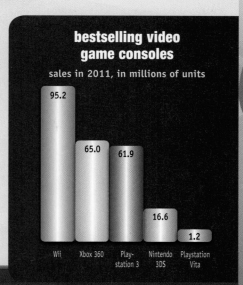

bestselling video game consoles

sales in 2011, in millions of units

Wii	95.2
Xbox 360	65.0
Play-station 3	61.9
Nintendo 3DS	16.6
Playstation Vita	1.2

fastest-selling family video game

POKÉMON DIAMOND/PEARL

Pokémon Diamond/Pearl is the fastest-selling family video game in history, moving 3.49 million units worldwide in just one week of 2006. Since the game debuted, it has sold more than 17.7 million units across the globe. Published by Nintendo, the Pokémon brand follows a Pokémon trainer who is preparing for battle. Diamond and Pearl features 493 Pokémon, including all the species from previous games and new species introduced for the first time. Pokémon—a combination of the words "pocket" and "monster"—is one of the best-selling game franchises in history.

fastest-selling family video games

sales in one week, in millions of units

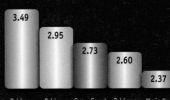

3.49	2.95	2.73	2.60	2.37
Pokémon Diamond/ Pearl	Pokémon Heart Gold/ Soul Silver	Super Smash Bros. Brawl	Pokémon Black/White	Mario Kart Wii

most-visited social site

Facebook

More than 137 million unique visitors click on the Facebook website each month. That's more than the next four social sites combined. Facebook was founded by Mark Zuckerberg in 2004 as a way for Harvard students to keep in touch. Seven years later, Facebook has more than 845 million active users monthly, and is available in 70 languages. The average user has 229 friends, and more than half of its users post status updates at least once a week. Over 700 billion minutes are spent on Facebook each month. In an average 2-minute time period, 1 million links are shared, another 2 million friend requests are accepted, and 3 million messages are sent.

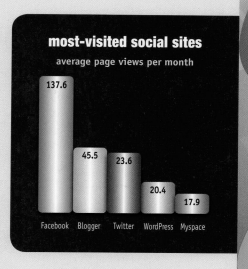

most-visited social sites

average page views per month

Facebook	Blogger	Twitter	WordPress	Myspace
137.6	45.5	23.6	20.4	17.9

most-visited website

GOOGLE

The most-visited website in the world is Google, which gets more than 153 million unique page views per month. Created by Stanford grad students Larry Page and Sergey Brin in 1998, Google indexed its 1 trillionth page by 2008. Google performs about 87 billion searches each month. There are also more than 350 million people using Gmail, the website's e-mail feature. Over the years, Google has acquired many impressive companies, including YouTube, Android, DoubleClick, and Blogger. Google employs about 20,000 people worldwide.

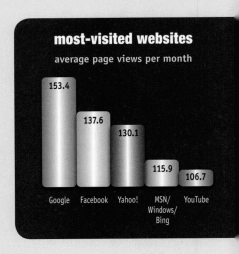

most-visited websites

average page views per month

Google	Facebook	Yahoo!	MSN/ Windows/ Bing	YouTube
153.4	137.6	130.1	115.9	106.7

most-visited search engine

GOOGLE

More than 63 percent of people browsing the Internet choose Google as their search engine. Google is the world's largest online index of websites. In addition, Google offers e-mail, maps, news, and financial services. Headquartered in California's Silicon Valley, the company runs more than one million servers and data centers around the globe. A "googol" is a 1 followed by 100 zeros, and the site was named after the term to indicate its mission to organize the virtually infinite amount of information on the web.

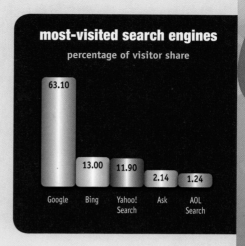

most-visited search engines

percentage of visitor share

Google	Bing	Yahoo! Search	Ask	AOL Search
63.10	13.00	11.90	2.14	1.24

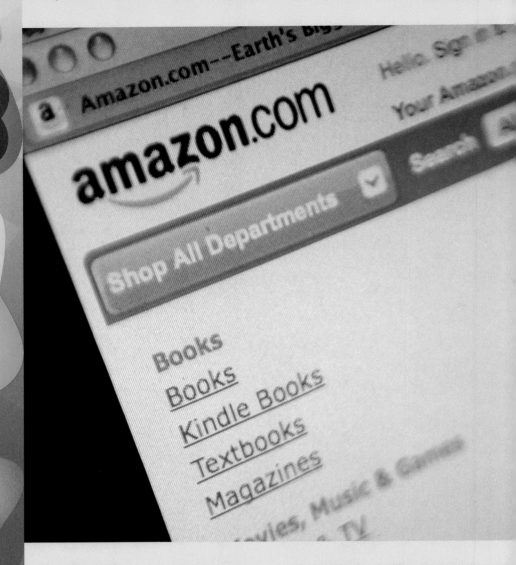

most-visited shopping site

AMAZON.COM

Shopping megasite Amazon.com has 282 million visitors browsing its products per month. The site, which got its start selling books, now offers everything from clothes and electronics to food and furniture. Founded by Jeffrey Bezos in 1994, it is headquartered in Seattle, Washington. The company also has separate websites in countries including Japan, Canada, the United Kingdom, Germany, and France.

most-visited shopping sites
number of visitors per month, in millions

282	224	157	134	58
Amazon	eBay	Alibaba	Apple	Rakulen

country with the most websites

GERMANY

There are 84.7 websites for every 1,000 people living in Germany. That means that there are about 7 million websites in the European country. Many websites originating from Germany end in ".de." There are more than 65.1 million Internet users in the country, which is about 79 percent of the population. That's the highest Internet usage in Europe. Germans ages 14 to 29 are the most likely to surf the web. The most popular websites in the country are very similar to those in the United States— they include Google, Facebook, YouTube, and eBay.

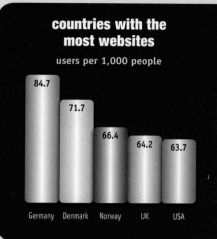

countries with the most websites

users per 1,000 people

Germany	Denmark	Norway	UK	USA
84.7	71.7	66.4	64.2	63.7

most popular facebook game

CITYVILLE

With more than 46 million registered players, CityVille is the most popular game on Facebook. The game was created by Zynga and lets players build the city of their dreams, while opening franchises, collecting rent, and arresting criminals along the way. And since the game is linked with other friends' Facebook accounts, players can work in one anothers' businesses. It is Zynga's first international game, and it debuted in five languages. Due to its great success, Zynga also developed CityVille Hometown, a smaller version of the game to be played on smartphones.

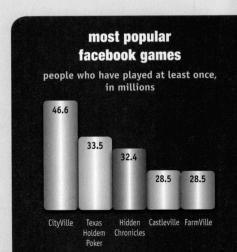

most popular facebook games

people who have played at least once, in millions

CityVille	Texas Holdem Poker	Hidden Chronicles	Castleville	FarmVille
46.6	33.5	32.4	28.5	28.5

product with the most facebook fans

coca-cola

Coca-Cola is the most popular product on Facebook with 40.3 million fans. On the page, fans can post and read stories, explore products, and check out the latest photos. The company has acquired some impressive statistics during its 125 years in business. Coca-Cola produces more than 3,500 different types of beverages, which are sold in 200 countries throughout the world. Each day, about 1.7 billion servings of Coca-Cola products are enjoyed. In addition to its cola products, the company also produces A&W, Crush, Dasani, Hi-C, Minute Maid, Nestea, and many others.

products with the most facebook fans

number of fans, in millions

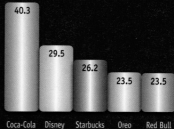

Coca-Cola	Disney	Starbucks	Oreo	Red Bull
40.3	29.5	26.2	23.5	23.5

most searched celebrity on google

JUSTIN BIEBER

Pop star Justin Bieber was the most searched celebrity on Google during 2011. The Canadian singer had a big year, releasing his second studio album—*Under the Mistletoe*—that debuted at the top of the Billboard 200 chart. He also released a 3-D biopic called *Justin Bieber: Never Say Never*, and it grossed more than $30 million in its first weekend. Bieber was ranked number two on *Forbes*'s Best-Paid Celebrities Under 30 list. At the Grammy Awards, Bieber was nominated for Best New Artist and Best Pop Vocal Album. At the end of 2011, the singer began recording his third studio album, *Believe*.

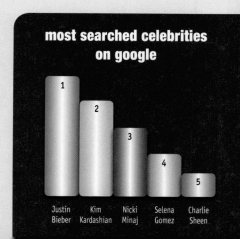

most searched celebrities on google

1	2	3	4	5
Justin Bieber	Kim Kardashian	Nicki Minaj	Selena Gomez	Charlie Sheen

most visited video site

YOUTUBE

When web surfers are looking for videos, the majority log on to YouTube. With more than 111 million unique page views per month, YouTube can turn everyday people into Internet stars. On the site, anyone can upload their own videos for the world to see. YouTube gets about 3 billion views per day. Each minute, about 48 hours of video is uploaded to the site. In fact, more video is uploaded to YouTube in one month than the three largest broadcast networks could create in 60 years. About 500 years' worth of YouTube video is shared on Facebook each day, and another 700 YouTube videos are shared on Twitter each minute.

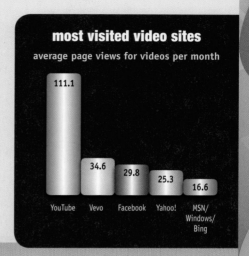

most visited video sites

average page views for videos per month

YouTube	111.1
Vevo	34.6
Facebook	29.8
Yahoo!	25.3
MSN/Windows/Bing	16.6

  Search Br

Animals That Do Exist

stevefowler   8 videos ⊻   Subscribe

AP / Gautam Singh

II 🔊   1:00 / 2:32   360p ↱

👍 Like 👎 + Add to ▾ Share ✉

4,633,455

Uploaded by stevefowler on Jul 12, 2007

They do

2,492 likes, 1,172 dislikes

Show more ▾

country with the most twitter accounts

USA

There are more than 107 million Twitter accounts in the United States. That's more than the next four top countries combined! In total, Twitter has 465 million accounts. Each day, about 1 million new Twitter accounts are opened—an average of 11.5 accounts per second. In just one week, approximately 1.2 billion tweets are sent out. About 40 percent of all users don't even tweet—they just follow others. And about half of all Twitter users access their accounts on their cell phones. Twitter was created in July 2006 by Jack Dorsey, Biz Stone, and Evan Williams.

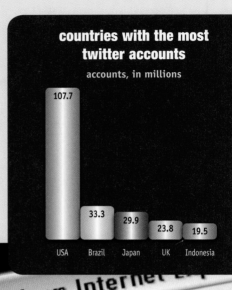

countries with the most twitter accounts

accounts, in millions

107.7	33.3	29.9	23.8	19.5
USA	Brazil	Japan	UK	Indonesia

celebrity with the most twitter followers

LADY GAGA

Lady Gaga's fans adore her, and more than 20 million of them follow her every tweet on Twitter. That's not the only social media site to get the latest Gaga news—she has 48 million fans on Facebook and more than 800,000 circles on Google+. She was the first celebrity to reach both 10 million and 15 million followers. And it took her only 23 days to go from 19 million to 20 million followers. In addition to reaching out to her "Little Monsters," Lady Gaga uses these sites to market her albums. Her latest album, *Born This Way*, has already sold 8 million copies.

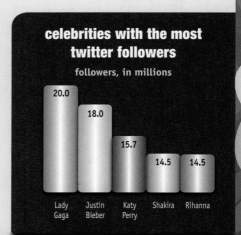

celebrities with the most twitter followers
followers, in millions

Lady Gaga	Justin Bieber	Katy Perry	Shakira	Rihanna
20.0	18.0	15.7	14.5	14.5

most active twitter moment

CASTLE IN THE SKY AIRING

The annual television screening of the 25-year-old animated Japanese film classic *Castle in the Sky* averaged 25,088 tweets per second! When *Castle in the Sky* aired in December 2011 in Japan, fans were encouraged to tweet the word "balse" to help Pazu and Sheeta—the main characters—cast a spell. Clearly fans responded. The film was created in Japan by Hayao Miyazaki and was released in 1986. It was later rereleased in English by Disney in 1999. The English version starred James Van Der Beek, Anna Paquin, Cloris Leachman, and Mark Hamill.

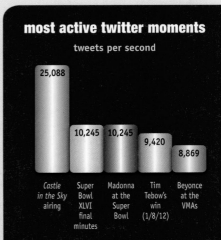

most active twitter moments

tweets per second

Castle in the Sky airing	Super Bowl XLVI final minutes	Madonna at the Super Bowl	Tim Tebow's win (1/8/12)	Beyonce at the VMAs
25,088	10,245	10,245	9,420	8,869

busiest retail e-mail day
CYBER MONDAY

About 87 percent of top Internet retailers sent out advertisements on November 28, 2011—also known as Cyber Monday. The Monday following the Thanksgiving weekend has traditionally become one of the biggest online shopping days as shoppers get a jump on the holiday purchases. In 2011, online shoppers spent more than $1 billion—up 22 percent from the previous year. This is the highest online shopping total in Internet history. The average online purchase set a record at $198. Almost 11 percent of online shoppers visited sites on their cell phones, and almost 7 percent of them made purchases.

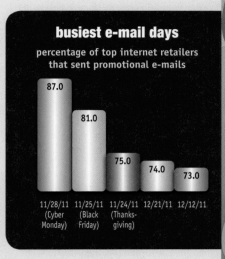

busiest e-mail days
percentage of top internet retailers that sent promotional e-mails

11/28/11 (Cyber Monday)	11/25/11 (Black Friday)	11/24/11 (Thanks-giving)	12/21/11	12/12/11
87.0	81.0	75.0	74.0	73.0

country with the highest internet usage

ICELAND

Iceland has the world's highest percentage of Internet users, with more than 97.8 percent of the country logging on to surf the web. That means about 302,000 people in the small European country have Internet access, and 98,000 are broadband subscribers. In comparison, only about 58 percent of the population in Europe as a whole goes online. Icelandic people mainly use the Internet to find information and to communicate, with about 45 percent of users also shopping online.

countries with the highest internet usage

percentage of population

Iceland	Norway	Sweden	Falkland Islands	Luxem-bourg
97.8	97.2	92.9	92.4	91.4

country with the most internet users

CHINa

China dominates the world in Internet usage, with 485 million people—or about one-third of the country—browsing the World Wide Web under government censorship. The number of Internet users in China has tripled in the last five years. About 250 million Internet users browse from their cell phones. These phone surfers account for much of the increase in Internet users. People spend an average of almost 20 hours a week online. Some Internet activities that are becoming increasingly popular in China include banking and booking travel.

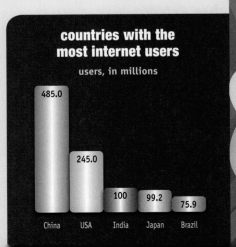

countries with the most internet users

users, in millions

China	USA	India	Japan	Brazil
485.0	245.0	100	99.2	75.9

bestselling cell phone brand

NOKIA

Nokia is the most popular cell phone brand worldwide and accounted for 27.0 percent of the market share—or total number of people buying cell phones—in 2011. Since launching its first mobile phone in 1992, the Finnish company has sold 460 million phones in 150 countries. Nokia introduced its first 3G phone in 2003, and went on to sell its 1 billionth phone in 2005. In 2007, Nokia's N95 became the first phone to combine GPS service and wireless broadband. The company operates 15 manufacturing plants across the globe, and employs 123,000 people.

bestselling cell phone brands

percentage of market share

Nokia	Samsung	Apple	LG Electronics	ZTE
27.0	21.3	6.0	5.7	4.3

anDroID

The Android maintains a slight lead in the country's smartphone race, with 40 percent of the market share. They are most popular with buyers ages 18 to 34, and men slightly outnumber women in ownership rates. On average, Android users have 22 apps. The top four apps of the Android are Google Maps, Facebook, the Weather Channel, and Pandora. And users remain loyal—more than 70 percent of current Android users intend to buy another when it comes time. More than 25 percent of all cell phone users now own a smartphone.

united states' bestselling smartphones

percentage of market share

Android	Apple	RIM Blackberry	Microsoft Windows Mobile	other
40	28	19	7	5

countries with the most mobile web users

ISraeL/JaPaN

Cell phone users in both Israel and Japan lead the world in web browsing, with 47 percent of mobile subscribers surfing the Internet on their phones. More than 80 percent of the Japanese population have cell phones, and they are much more popular than landlines. Most phones in the country operate on a 3G network, making web surfing easy. In Israel, about 95 percent of the population use a cell phone, and about 53 percent of them use it to log on to social networking sites. This is most common with Israelis ages 18 to 29.

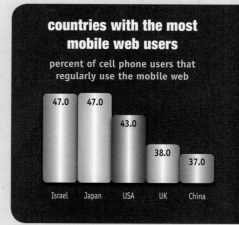

countries with the most mobile web users

percent of cell phone users that regularly use the mobile web

Israel	Japan	USA	UK	China
47.0	47.0	43.0	38.0	37.0

bestselling app type

GAMES

Games are the top app choice among smartphone users, with about 67 percent of users downloading them. The bestselling iPhone games include Angry Birds, Fruit Ninja, and Doodle Jump. Some of the most popular Android games include World of Goo, Scribblenauts Remix, and Tiny Tower. More than 25 percent of adults download apps regularly, and the average user has about 18 of them. More than 300,000 mobile apps have been developed in the last three years, and a total of 10.9 billion have been downloaded. About 1.2 billion apps were downloaded between Christmas and New Year's 2011 alone.

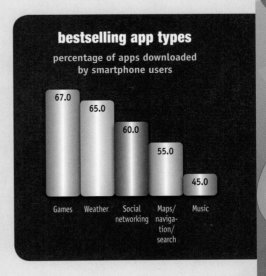

bestselling app types

percentage of apps downloaded by smartphone users

Games	Weather	Social networking	Maps/ navigation/ search	Music
67.0	65.0	60.0	55.0	45.0

country that watches the most tv

UNITED STATES

The United States likes to watch a lot of television, averaging 33 hours of weekly program viewing per capita. That's the equivalent of more than 71 straight days, or 2 months per year. Ninety-eight percent of American households own at least one television, and about 54 percent of children have a set in their bedrooms. About 6 percent of families watch TV while eating dinner, and about 70 percent of day-care centers use televisions as well. Each year, kids watch about 20,000 30-second commercials, which increases to 2 million by the time they are 65.

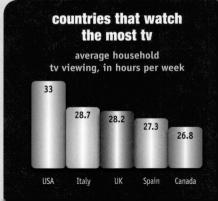

countries that watch the most tv

average household
tv viewing, in hours per week

USA	Italy	UK	Spain	Canada
33	28.7	28.2	27.3	26.8

largest cruise ships

OASIS OF THE SEAS & ALLURE OF THE SEAS

Royal Caribbean's sister cruise ships—*Oasis of the Seas* and *Allure of the Seas*—weigh in at 225,282 gross tons (228,897 t) each! These giant ships are more like floating cities with seven different themed neighborhoods: Central Park, Boardwalk, Royal Promenade, Pool and Sports Zone, Vitality at Sea Spa and Fitness Center, Entertainment Place, and Youth Zone. *Oasis of the Seas* and *Allure of the Seas* each span 16 decks and include more than 20 eateries, 3 pools, a water park, and a zip-line ride. Both ships have 2,700 staterooms and can accommodate a whopping 5,400 guests.

largest cruise ships

weight, in gross tons (tonnes)

Oasis of the Seas	Allure of the Seas	Independence of the Seas	Liberty of the Seas	Freedom of the Seas
225,282 (228,897)	225,282 (228,897)	160,000 (162,567)	160,000 (162,567)	160,000 (162,567)

Oasis of the Seas

Royal Caribbean
INTERNATIONAL

fastest passenger train

CRH380AL

When China unveiled the CRH380AL commercial passenger train in 2010, it cruised into the record books with a top speed of 302 miles (486 km) per hour. The train reached its top speed in just 22 minutes. The train route connects Beijing and Shanghai, and will reduce the average travel time from 10 hours to 4 hours. The train is expected to carry about 80 million people along the 818-mile (1,316 km) route. The new train is part of China's $313 billion program to develop the world's most advanced train system by 2020.

fastest passenger trains

maximum speed, in miles (kilometers) per hour

302 (486)	259 (417)	251 (404)	245 (394)	217 (349)
CRH380AL, China	CRH380A, China	AVE-S 103, Germany	CRH3, China	700T, Japan

biggest monster truck

BIGFOOT 5

The Bigfoot 5 truly is a monster—it measures 15.4 feet (4.7 m) high! That's about three times the height of an average car. Bigfoot 5 has 10-foot (3 m) Firestone Tundra tires, each weighing 2,400 pounds (1,088 kg), giving the truck a total weight of about 38,000 pounds (17,236 kg). The giant wheels were from an arctic snow train operated in Alaska by the US Army in the 1950s. This modified 1996 Ford F250 pickup truck is owned by Bob Chandler of St. Louis, Missouri. The great weight of this monster truck makes it too large to race.

biggest monster trucks
height, in feet (meters)

Bigfoot 5	Big Pete	Mass Destruction	Fat Landy	Black Widow
15.4 (4.7)	15.0 (4.6)	14.2 (4.3)	12.8 (3.9)	12.0 (3.7)

smallest car

Peel P50

The Peel P50 is the smallest production car ever made, measuring just 4.25 feet (1.3 m) long. That's not much longer than the average adult bicycle! The Peel P50 was produced in the Isle of Man between 1962 and 1965, and only 46 cars were made. It is just big enough to hold one adult and one bag. The Peel P50 has three wheels, one door, one windshield wiper, and one headlight, and was available in red, white, or blue. The microcar weighs just 130 pounds (58.9 kg) and measures about 4 feet (1.2 m) tall. With its three-speed manual transmission, it can reach a top speed of 38 miles (61 km) an hour. However, it cannot go in reverse.

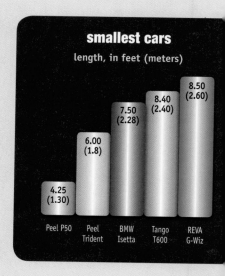

smallest cars

length, in feet (meters)

4.25 (1.30)	6.00 (1.8)	7.50 (2.28)	8.40 (2.40)	8.50 (2.60)
Peel P50	Peel Trident	BMW Isetta	Tango T600	REVA G-Wiz

fastest land vehicle

THRUST SSC

The Thrust SSC, which stands for Supersonic Car, reached a speed of 763 miles (1,228 km) per hour on October 15, 1997. At that speed, a car could make it from San Francisco to New York City in less than four hours. The Thrust SSC is propelled by two jet engines capable of 110,000 horsepower. It has the same power as 1,000 Ford Escorts or 145 Formula One race cars. The Thrust SSC runs on jet fuel, using about 5 gallons (19 L) per second. It takes only approximately five seconds for this supersonic car to reach its top speed. It is 54 feet (16.5 m) long and weighs 7 tons (6.4 t).

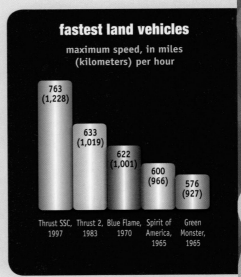

fastest land vehicles

maximum speed, in miles (kilometers) per hour

Thrust SSC, 1997	Thrust 2, 1983	Blue Flame, 1970	Spirit of America, 1965	Green Monster, 1965
763 (1,228)	633 (1,019)	622 (1,001)	600 (966)	576 (927)

fastest production motorcycle

DUCATI DESMOSEDICI RR

The Ducati Desmosedici RR can speed down the street at 196 miles (315 km) per hour. That's about three times the speed limit on most US highways! This Italian street bike, which was originally created to race in the MotoGP World Championships, can accelerate from 0 to 60 miles (96 km) per hour in just 2.43 seconds. The liquid-cooled, 16-valve engine has four cylinders with gear-driven crankshafts. The Desmosedici uses Bridgestone tires and Brembo brakes. Only 1,500 of these special bikes were created, and the base price for each is $72,500.

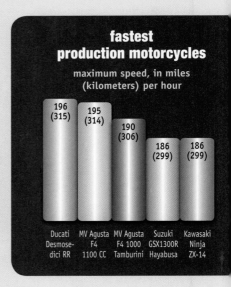

fastest production motorcycles

maximum speed, in miles (kilometers) per hour

Ducati Desmosedici RR	MV Agusta F4 1100 CC	MV Agusta F4 1000 Tamburini	Suzuki GSX1300R Hayabusa	Kawasaki Ninja ZX-14
196 (315)	195 (314)	190 (306)	186 (299)	186 (299)

fastest production car

BUGATTI VEYRON 16.4 SUPER SPORT

With a top cruising speed of 267 miles (430 km) per hour, the Bugatti Veyron 16.4 Super Sport is the fastest production car in the world. It can cruise at more than four times the average speed limit on most highways! The Super Sport has a sleek, aerodynamic design that feeds air to the 16-cylinder engine from the roof, rather than just above the hood. The shell of the car is made of carbon-fiber composites to make the car lighter, while maintaining its safety. The Super Sport debuted at the Pebble Beach Concourse in August 2010.

fastest production cars

maximum speed, in miles (kilometers) per hour

Bugatti Veyron 16.4 Super Sport	Hennessey Venom GT	Koenigsegg Agera R	SSC Ultimate Aero	Saleen S7 Twin Turbo
267 (430)	260 (418)	260 (418)	257 (414)	248 (399)

fastest traditional helicopter

SIKORSKY X-2

The Sikorsky X-2 experimental compound helicopter reached a top speed of 287 miles (462 km) per hour in September 2010. The successful flight lasted just over one hour. Sikorsky was able to accomplish this record-breaking speed in 17 test flights with just over 16 flight hours. The company made several improvements to the original X-2—including reducing the drag, implementing rigid rotor blades, and finalizing vibration control—to achieve its success. Sikorsky continues to experiment with the X-2 to increase speed and performance for future models to be used by the military.

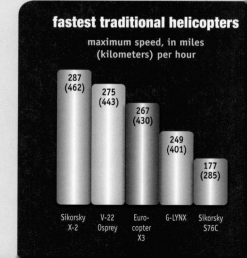

fastest traditional helicopters
maximum speed, in miles (kilometers) per hour

Sikorsky X-2	V-22 Osprey	Euro-copter X3	G-LYNX	Sikorsky S76C
287 (462)	275 (443)	267 (430)	249 (401)	177 (285)

lightest jet

BD-5J MICROJET

The BD-5J Microjet weighs only 358.8 pounds (162.7 kg), making it the lightest jet in the world. At only 12 feet (3.7 m) in length, it is one of the smallest as well. This tiny jet has a height of 5.6 feet (1.7 m) and a wingspan of 17 feet (5.2 m). The Microjet uses a TRS-18 turbojet engine. It can reach a top speed of 320 miles (514.9 km) per hour, but can carry only 32 gallons (121 L) of fuel at a time. A new BD-5J costs around $200,000. This high-tech gadget was flown by James Bond in the movie *Octopussy*, and it is also occasionally used by the US military.

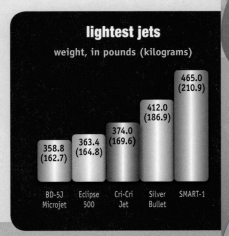

lightest jets

weight, in pounds (kilograms)

BD-5J Microjet	Eclipse 500	Cri-Cri Jet	Silver Bullet	SMART-1
358.8 (162.7)	363.4 (164.8)	374.0 (169.6)	412.0 (186.9)	465.0 (210.9)

fastest plane

X-43a

NASA's experimental X-43A plane reached a top speed of Mach 9.8—or more than nine times the speed of sound—on a test flight over the Pacific Ocean in November 2004. The X-43A was mounted on top of a Pegasus rocket booster and was carried into the sky by a B-52 aircraft. The booster was then fired, taking the X-43A about 110,000 feet (33,530 m) above the ground. The rocket was detached from the unmanned X-43A, and the plane flew unassisted for several minutes. At this rate of 7,459 miles (12,004 km) per hour, a plane could circle Earth in just over three and a half hours!

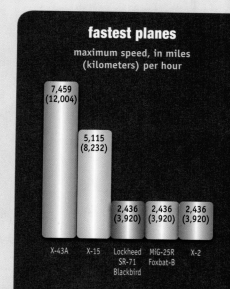

fastest planes

maximum speed, in miles (kilometers) per hour

X-43A	X-15	Lockheed SR-71 Blackbird	MiG-25R Foxbat-B	X-2
7,459 (12,004)	5,115 (8,232)	2,436 (3,920)	2,436 (3,920)	2,436 (3,920)

tallest roller coaster
KINGDA KA

Kingda Ka towers over Six Flags Great Adventure in Jackson, New Jersey, at a height of 456 feet (139 m). Its highest drop plummets riders down 418 feet (127 m). The steel coaster can reach a top speed of 128 miles (206 km) per hour in just 3.5 seconds, and it was the fastest coaster in the world when it opened in 2005. The entire 3,118-foot (950 m) ride is over in just 28 seconds. The hydraulic launch coaster is located in the Golden Kingdom section of the park. It can accommodate about 1,400 riders per hour.

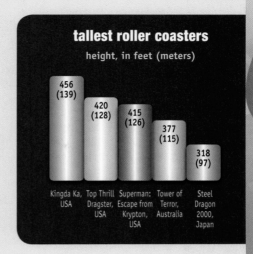

tallest roller coasters
height, in feet (meters)

Kingda Ka, USA	Top Thrill Dragster, USA	Superman: Escape from Krypton, USA	Tower of Terror, Australia	Steel Dragon 2000, Japan
456 (139)	420 (128)	415 (126)	377 (115)	318 (97)

amusement park with the most rides

cedar POINT

Located in Sandusky, Ohio, Cedar Point offers park visitors 73 rides to enjoy. Windseeker—the park's newest ride—is a 300-foot (91 m) swing above Cedar Point Beach. Top Thrill Dragster roller coaster is the second tallest in the world at 420 feet (128 m). And with 17 roller coasters, Cedar Point also has the most coasters of any theme park in the world. Over 53,963 feet (16,448 m) of coaster track—more than 10 miles (16.1 km)—run through the park. In 2008, Cedar Point was named Best Amusement Park in the World by *Amusement Today* for the 11th time.

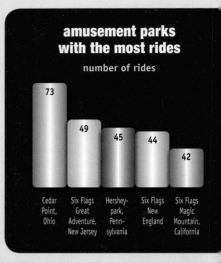

amusement parks with the most rides

number of rides

Cedar Point, Ohio	Six Flags Great Adventure, New Jersey	Hersheypark, Pennsylvania	Six Flags New England	Six Flags Magic Mountain, California
73	49	45	44	42

fastest roller coaster

Formula rossa

The Formula Rossa coaster in the United Arab Emirates speeds past the competition with a top speed of 149 miles (240 km) per hour. Located at Ferrari World in Dubai, riders climb into the F1 race car cockpits and can experience what 4.8 g-force actually feels like. The coaster's hydraulic launch system rockets the coaster to its top speed in just 4.9 seconds. The track is about 1.4 miles (2.2 km) long, with the sharpest turn measuring 70 degrees. To protect riders' eyes from flying insects, safety goggles must be worn throughout the ride.

fastest roller coasters

speed, in miles (kilometers) per hour

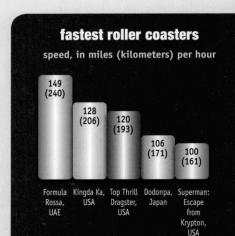

Formula Rossa, UAE	Kingda Ka, USA	Top Thrill Dragster, USA	Dodonpa, Japan	Superman: Escape from Krypton, USA
149 (240)	128 (206)	120 (193)	106 (171)	100 (161)

city with the most skyscrapers

NEW YORK

New York City has the most skyscrapers in the world with 210 buildings reaching 500 feet (152 m) or higher. The three tallest buildings in the Big Apple are the Empire State Building at 1,250 feet (381 m), the Bank of America Tower at 1,200 feet (366 m), and the Chrysler Building at 1,046 feet (318 m). The first skyscrapers popped up in New York City in the mid-1890s. With more than 22.1 million people currently living in the metropolitan area, architects had to continue building up instead of out. In the last 200 years, New York City has held the record for the world's tallest building 11 times.

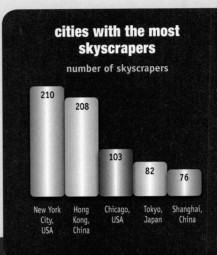

cities with the most skyscrapers
number of skyscrapers

New York City, USA	Hong Kong, China	Chicago, USA	Tokyo, Japan	Shanghai, China
210	208	103	82	76

tallest habitable building

BURJ KHALIFA

Burj Khalifa in the United Arab Emirates towers 2,716 feet (828 m) above the ground. With more than 160 floors, the building cost about $4.1 billion to construct. Both a hotel and apartments are housed inside the luxury building, which covers 500 acres (202 ha). The building features high-speed elevators, traveling at 40 miles (64 km) per hour. The tower supplies its occupants with about 250,000 gallons (66,043 L) of water a day, and delivers enough electricity to power 360,000 100-watt lightbulbs.

tallest habitable buildings

height, in feet (meters)

Burj Khalifa, UAE	Taipei 101, Taiwan	Shanghai World Financial Center, China	International Commerce Centre, Hong Kong	Petronas Twin Towers, Malaysia
2,716 (828)	1,666 (508)	1,614 (492)	1,588 (484)	1,483 (452)

largest swimming pool

san alfonso del mar

The gigantic swimming pool at the San Alfonso del Mar resort, in Chile, spreads over 19.7 acres (8 ha). The monstrous pool is the equivalent to 6,000 standard swimming pools and holds 66 million gallons (250 million L) of water. In addition to swimming, guests can sail and scuba dive in the saltwater lagoon, which is surrounded by white sand beaches. And no diving for pennies here—the deep end measures 115 feet (35 m). The pool took five years to complete and first opened in December 2006. The project cost $2 billion, and costs about $4 million annually to maintain it.

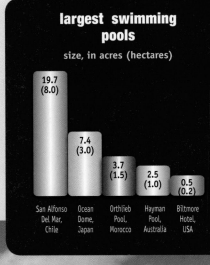

largest swimming pools

size, in acres (hectares)

19.7 (8.0)	7.4 (3.0)	3.7 (1.5)	2.5 (1.0)	0.5 (0.2)
San Alfonso Del Mar, Chile	Ocean Dome, Japan	Orthlieb Pool, Morocco	Hayman Pool, Australia	Biltmore Hotel, USA

largest sports stadium

RUNGRADO MAY FIRST STADIUM

The Rungrado May First Stadium, also known as the May Day Stadium, can seat up to 150,000 people. The interior of the stadium covers 2.2 million square feet (204,386 sq m). Located in Pyongyang, North Korea, this venue is mostly used for soccer matches and other athletic contests. It is named after Rungra Island, on which the stadium is located, in the middle of the Taedong River. When it is not being used for sporting events, the stadium is used for a two-month festival known as Arirang.

largest sports stadiums
number of seats

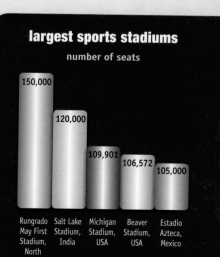

Stadium	Number of seats
Rungrado May First Stadium, North Korea	150,000
Salt Lake Stadium, India	120,000
Michigan Stadium, USA	109,901
Beaver Stadium, USA	106,572
Estadio Azteca, Mexico	105,000

busiest airport

HARTSFIELD-JACKSON ATLANTA INTERNATIONAL AIRPORT

The Hartsfield-Jackson Atlanta International Airport serves more than 92 million travelers in one year. That's more people than are living in California, Texas, and Florida combined. Approximately 967,050 planes depart and arrive at this airport every year. With parking lots, runways, maintenance facilities, and other buildings, the Hartsfield terminal complex covers about 130 acres (53 ha). Hartsfield-Jackson Atlanta International Airport has a north and a south terminal, an underground train, and six concourses with a total of 154 domestic and 28 international gates.

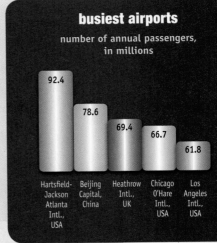

busiest airports
number of annual passengers, in millions

Hartsfield-Jackson Atlanta Intl., USA	Beijing Capital, China	Heathrow Intl., UK	Chicago O'Hare Intl., USA	Los Angeles Intl., USA
92.4	78.6	69.4	66.7	61.8

country that produces the most cars

CHINA

China leads the world in car production by creating 13.8 million vehicles annually. Approximately 44 percent of all the cars produced in the country are Chinese brands, including Lifan, Geely, Chery, and several others. International brands with factories in China include Volkswagen, General Motors, and Honda. Most of the cars that are produced in China are also sold there. Fewer than 400,000 cars are exported each year. China's growth in the car production industry is fairly recent. Since the country joined the World Trade Organization in 2001, China's car production has grown by about 1 million vehicles annually.

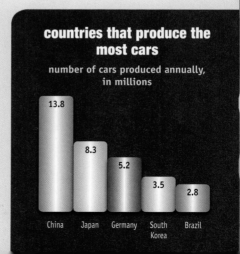

countries that produce the most cars

number of cars produced annually, in millions

China	Japan	Germany	South Korea	Brazil
13.8	8.3	5.2	3.5	2.8

city with the busiest subway system

TOKYO

Every year, more than 3 billion riders pack into the Tokyo subway. The system operates more than 2,500 cars and 282 subway stations. The tracks run for 175 miles (281 km). The Tokyo underground railroad opened in 1927. It has expanded through the years to include nine subway lines that connect the bustling areas of Chiyoda, Minato, and Chuo. The Tokyo Metro has recently taken steps to upgrade its cars and stations, reinforcing car frames and redesigning station platforms.

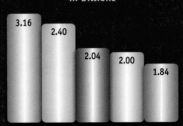

cities with the busiest subway systems

number of annual passengers, in billions

Tokyo, Japan	Moscow, Russia	Seoul, South Korea	Shanghai, China	Beijing, China
3.16	2.40	2.04	2.00	1.84

greenest city

reYKJaVíK

The Icelandic city of Reykjavík was ranked the greenest city in the world by *GlobalPost* because of its commitment to reducing its carbon footprint and its pledge to improve the environment. Reykjavík runs almost entirely on geothermal power and hydroelectricity. In its quest to become the most environmentally responsible city in Europe, Reykjavík uses only hydrogen-powered buses. The university has also begun integrating environmental issues and sustainability into most classes. The city is made up of about 170,000 people, which is about 60 percent of the country's population.

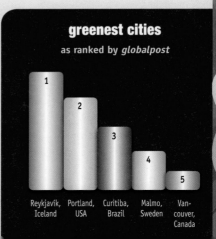

greenest cities
as ranked by *globalpost*

1	2	3	4	5
Reykjavík, Iceland	Portland, USA	Curitiba, Brazil	Malmo, Sweden	Van-couver, Canada

MONEY
records

most expensive ○ most valuable ○ big business

DIGITAL DOLLARS

The most valuable digital start-up company in the world is Facebook, which was valued at more than $110 billion when the company went public in May 2012. About 850 million people around the world use Facebook, and that number is expected to reach 1 billion by 2013.

COSTLY KITTY

When Sanrio celebrated Hello Kitty's 35th birthday in 2009, they teamed up with crystal maker Swarovski to create a special doll. The platinum-based doll is 4 inches (10 cm) tall and covered with 1,939 pieces of white topaz, 403 pink sapphires, and a 1-carat diamond bow. The pricey feline is worth $167,000.

CHEAP AS DIRT

Baseball fans with an extra $89.95 can buy a teaspoon of dirt from the old Yankee Stadium. The dirt was used on the field during the last game played at the stadium on September 21, 2008, when the Yankees beat the Baltimore Orioles. The dirt was pressed into the shape of a coin, and mounted on a plaque with a photo of the stadium.

BIG BUCKS IN BASKETBALL

The Louisville Cardinals at the University of Louisville in Kentucky are the NCAA's most valuable basketball team with a total worth of $36.1 million. In addition to ticket and concession sales, most revenue is brought in by monetary contributions that are required before fans are allowed to purchase season tickets. Only 5 other NCAA teams were able to generate $20 million in revenue.

THE WRITE STUFF

The most expensive author signature in the world belongs to William Shakespeare, and it's valued at $3 million. Shakespeare's signatures are so valuable because there are just six known in the world—three on his will, two on housing documents, and one on a legal document.

COSTLY COLLECTION

Legendary actress Elizabeth Taylor's extravagant jewelry collection was auctioned off for a record $137.2 million in December 2011. Every piece of jewelry in the 190-item collection was sold in about 8 hours, and many went for more than 10 times the estimated price.

BIG BUCKS BID

Edvard Munch's most famous painting—*The Scream*—shattered auction records in May 2012 when it sold for $119.9 million. Bidding started at $40 million and took about 12 minutes to reach the selling price. In addition to the painting, the winner also got a poem written by Munch explaining the inspiration for the painting.

most expensive hotel

roYaL PenTHouSe SuiTe

Guests better bring their wallets to the President Wilson Hotel in Geneva, Switzerland—the Royal Penthouse Suite costs $65,000 a night! That means a weeklong stay would total $455,000, which is almost twice the price of buying the average house in the US. The suite is reserved for heads of state and celebrities, and offers beautiful views of the Alps and Lake Geneva. The 18,082-square-foot (1,680 sq m) four-bedroom luxury suite has a private elevator and marble bathrooms. The state-of-the-art security system includes bulletproof doors and windows.

most expensive hotels

cost per night, in US dollars

65,000	50,000	45,000	41,800	35,000
Royal Penthouse Suite, President Wilson Hotel, Switzerland	Royal Villa, Grand Resort Lagonessi, Greece	Presidential Suite, Raj Palace, India	Ty Warner Penthouse, Four Seasons, USA	Hugh Hefner Sky Villa, Palms Casino & Resort, USA

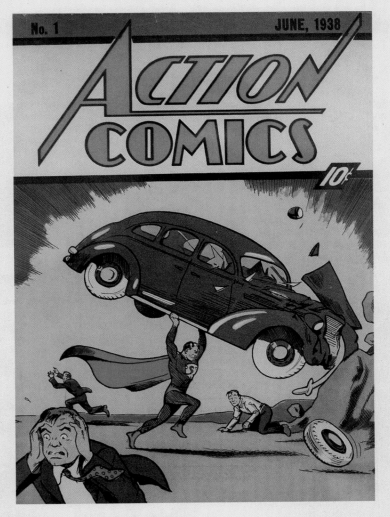

most expensive comic book

ACTION COMICS, NO. 1

Action Comics, No. 1 sold for $2.1 million at auction in November 2011. This comic was published in April 1938 and introduced Superman to the world. Known as the world's first superhero comic, it featured the Man of Steel lifting up a car on its cover. It originally sold for 10 cents. Comic artists Jerry Siegel and Joe Shuster created the book and were paid $10 per page. About 200,000 copies were printed, but only about 100 survive today. Another copy of the same issue was auctioned off in March 2010, but fetched only $1.5 million because it was not in as good condition.

most expensive comic books
price, in US dollars

2.16M	1.50M	1.38M	1.00M	671,000
Action Comics, No. 1	Action Comics, No. 1	Detective Comics, No. 27	Action Comics, No. 1	Superman, No. 1

most expensive bicycle

"BUTTERFLY" TREK MADONE

The "Butterfly" Trek Madone bike sold for $500,000 at a Sotheby's auction that raised money for the Lance Armstrong Foundation to fight cancer. The bike, ridden by Lance Armstrong in the final leg of the 2009 Tour de France, was designed by artist Damien Hurst. He used hundreds of real butterfly wings and pink LIVESTRONG logos to decorate the frame and rims of the bike. There was some controversy over the creation of this bike when PETA (People for the Ethical Treatment of Animals) raised concerns about real animals being used for decoration. A basic Trek Madone costs about $4,000.

most expensive bicycles

price, in US dollars

"Butter-fly" Trek Madone	Trek Yoshitomo Nara Speed Concept	Aurumania Crystal Edition Gold Bike	Trek Madone 7-Diamond	Montante Luxury Gold Collection
500,000	200,000	101,000	75,000	46,000

most expensive production car

BUGATTI VEYRON 16.4 SUPER SPORT

The Bugatti Veyron Super Sport costs a cool $2.6 million. The basic model of this pricey machine debuted in 2005, and the Super Sport edition was introduced in 2010. The Veyron Super Sport has some impressive specifications, including 1,200 horsepower. The car also features a twin clutch gearbox with seven speeds, and the four enlarged superchargers boost the powerful 16-valve engine. Only 30 Veyron Super Sports will be produced as they are ordered. The first 5 will be orange and black, which is the same color scheme of the prototype used to introduce the model.

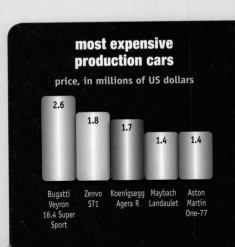

most expensive production cars

price, in millions of US dollars

Bugatti Veyron 16.4 Super Sport	Zenvo ST1	Koenigsegg Agera R	Maybach Landaulet	Aston Martin One-77
2.6	1.8	1.7	1.4	1.4

most expensive jewelry sold at auction

THE GRAFF PINK

Upon purchasing the 24.78-carat diamond for $46.2 million at a Sotheby's auction in 2010, jeweler Laurence Graff called it "the most fabulous diamond I've seen in my career." Jeweler Harry Winston once owned the fabulous gem, but the new owner renamed the ring the Graff Pink after himself. Graff owns the second-most-expensive diamond as well. The Graff Pink is very rare due to its deep color and purity. It was classified as "fancy intense pink"—the most perfect pink rating—by the Gemological Institute of America and categorized as potentially flawless.

most expensive jewelry sold at auction

price at auction, in millions of US dollars

Graff Pink diamond ring	Wittels-bach-Graff diamond	The Perfect Pink diamond ring	Bulgari two-stone diamond ring	Wallis Simpson's Panther bracelet
46.2	24.3	23.2	15.7	12.4

most valuable sports brand

NIKE

The Nike brand is worth more than $15 billion worldwide. Nike leads the footwear industry with 38 percent of the market. In 2012, Nike signed a deal to become the official licensed-apparel maker of the NFL for the next five years. During 2011, Nike earned more than $20.8 billion. The company was founded in 1972 by Bill Bowerman and Phil Knight, and it has grown to include many successful subsidiaries such as Converse, Umbro, and Cole Haan. Nike operates in 160 countries across six continents and employs 35,000 people.

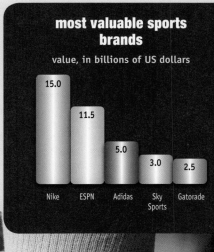

most valuable sports brands

value, in billions of US dollars

Nike	ESPN	Adidas	Sky Sports	Gatorade
15.0	11.5	5.0	3.0	2.5

most valuable

most valuable football team

DALLAS COWBOYS

Worth $1.85 billion, the Dallas Cowboys are the most valuable team in the National Football League for the fifth year in a row. In addition to ticket sales, the Cowboys have several side businesses that bring in the cash. In 2008, they launched Legends Hospitality Management, a company that consults with other team owners to maximize earnings. They also started Silver Star Merchandising to make and distribute team apparel. Cowboy Stadium has 320 suites and 15,000 club seats, and generates $115 million in revenue annually. The team and its loyal fans have enjoyed 21 division championships, 10 conference championships, and 5 Super Bowl championships since the franchise began in 1960.

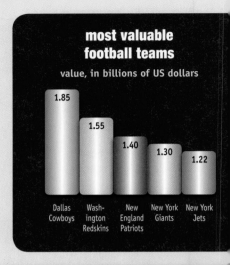

most valuable football teams

value, in billions of US dollars

Dallas Cowboys	Wash-ington Redskins	New England Patriots	New York Giants	New York Jets
1.85	1.55	1.40	1.30	1.22

most valuable hockey team
TORONTO MAPLE LEAFS

The Toronto Maple Leafs are worth a whopping $521 million, which is $281 million more than the average pro hockey team's value. The team's top ranking is largely due to strong ticket sales and lucrative television deals. Although Toronto won 13 Stanley Cups between 1917 and 1967, they have not won a cup in 45 years, which is the longest losing streak in the league. Toronto was one of the six teams that formed the National Hockey League in 1917. Their home arena is called Air Canada Centre.

most valuable hockey teams
value, in millions of US dollars

Toronto Maple Leafs	New York Rangers	Montreal Canadiens	Detroit Red Wings	Boston Bruins
521	507	445	336	325

soccer team with the highest revenue

real madrid

Spain's Real Madrid Football Club brought in $695 million in revenue during the 2011–2012 season. Founded in 1902, Real Madrid has won the European Cup a record nine times. The team has some huge stars, such as Ronaldo, who help sell tons of Real Madrid merchandise to enthusiastic fans around the world. In addition to ticket and merchandise sales, the team earns a great deal of money from television stations that air their matches. Worth about $1.4 billion, Real Madrid is the second most valuable team in the world.

soccer teams with the highest revenue

revenue, in millions of US dollars

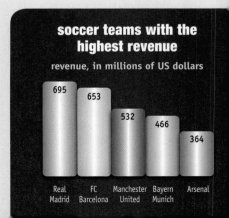

Real Madrid	FC Barcelona	Manchester United	Bayern Munich	Arsenal
695	653	532	466	364

LOS ANGELES LAKERS

The Los Angeles Lakers are worth about $900 million. The team brought in $208 million in revenue, and another $24.3 million in operating income during the 2011 season. A lucrative television deal also added to their value. One of the most successful teams in the league, the Lakers won 31 conference titles and 16 NBA championships between 1949 and 2010. They also hold the record for the longest winning streak with 33 games during the 1971–1972 season. Some of the game's top players have worn the Lakers uniform, including Kareem Abdul-Jabbar, Magic Johnson, Shaquille O'Neal, and Kobe Bryant.

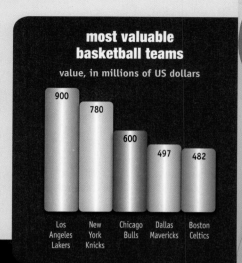

most valuable basketball teams

value, in millions of US dollars

Los Angeles Lakers	New York Knicks	Chicago Bulls	Dallas Mavericks	Boston Celtics
900	780	600	497	482

Ford F-series

Ford sold 584,917 F-Series trucks during 2011. The F-Series originated in 1948, when the F-1 (half ton), the F-2 (three-quarter ton), and the F-3 (Heavy Duty) were introduced. Since then, many modifications and new editions have been introduced, including the F-150. The modern F-150 sports a V-8 engine and the option of a regular, extended, or crew cab. The bed size ranges from 5.5 feet (1.6 m) to 8 feet (2.4 km). The Platinum F-150—the top-of-the-line version—features platinum chrome wheels, a fancy grille design, leather upholstery, and heated seats.

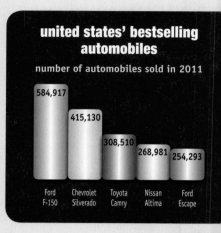

united states' bestselling automobiles

number of automobiles sold in 2011

Ford F-150	Chevrolet Silverado	Toyota Camry	Nissan Altima	Ford Escape
584,917	415,130	308,510	268,981	254,293

largest global retailer

walmart

Megadiscount retail chain Walmart had more than $421 billion in sales during 2011. Walmart serves more than 200 million customers each week at its more than 9,600 stores. Located in 28 countries, the company employs more than 1.4 million people in the United States and another 700,000 worldwide. This makes Walmart one of the largest private employers in North America. Walmart also believes in giving back to the community and donated more than $732 million to local charities in 2011. Walmart is currently ranked number one in the Fortune 500 list of most profitable companies.

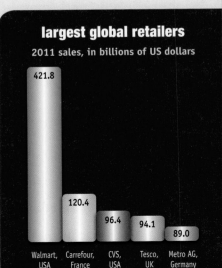

largest global retailers

2011 sales, in billions of US dollars

Walmart, USA	Carrefour, France	CVS, USA	Tesco, UK	Metro AG, Germany
421.8	120.4	96.4	94.1	89.0

largest global food franchise

SUBWAY

There are 33,959 Subway restaurants located throughout the world. There are 23,850 franchises in the United States, and another 10,109 international locations. Subway, which is owned by Doctor's Associates, Inc., had global sales totaling $15.2 billion in 2011—up about 10 percent from the previous year. The sandwich company was started by Fred DeLuca in 1965, and began franchising in 1974. Start-up fees run between $84,000 and $258,000, and 100 percent of the company is franchised. About 65 percent of franchises own more than one location.

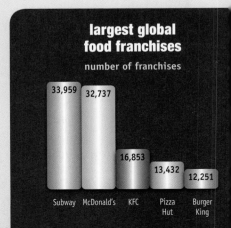

largest global food franchises
number of franchises

Subway	McDonald's	KFC	Pizza Hut	Burger King
33,959	32,737	16,853	13,432	12,251

largest retail franchise

7-ELEVEN

There are 39,482 7-Eleven convenience stores located around the world. Approximately 96 percent of these stores are franchised, with 6,137 locations in the United States and 33,345 locations internationally. 7-Eleven earned $63 billion in sales in 2011. The store chain is ranked number two on the *Forbes* Top Franchise for the Money list, meaning that investors have a very good chance of making a profit on their stores. The stores sell about 275 baked goods every minute, more than 2,300 fresh sandwiches each hour, and 13 million Slurpee beverages each month. Approximately 25 percent of Americans live within a mile (1.6 km) of a 7-Eleven store.

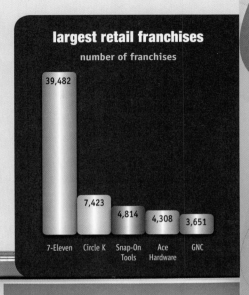

largest retail franchises

number of franchises

7-Eleven	Circle K	Snap-On Tools	Ace Hardware	GNC
39,482	7,423	4,814	4,308	3,651

POP CULTURE

records

books ● television ● movies ● music ● theater

HUNGRY FOR TICKETS

In February 2012, *The Hunger Games* set a record for the most pre-sale tickets sold by any movie in Fandango history. The movie accounted for about 83 percent of ticket sales on the first day that tickets were available, and many premieres were sold out more than a month in advance. More than 30 million people have read the book version of the trilogy, written by Suzanne Collins.

NUMBER ONE IN NOMINATIONS

In 2011, *Saturday Night Live* became the most nominated program in Emmy Award history with 142. The comedy sketch program received its first nominations during its debut year in 1976. *SNL* also set a record in 2011 for the most nominations for a variety show, with 16 nods.

LADY'S FIRST

Lady Antebellum finished 2011 as the music industry's best-selling group, with 2.1 million albums sold. They held this record the previous year as well, but Metallica's self-titled album holds the all-time sales record with 15.7 million units sold.

STREAMING TO THE TOP

The titles of most streamed song and most streamed video both belong to Nicki Minaj's "Super Bass." The song was streamed 84.9 million times in 2011, and the video was streamed 71 million times. Minaj co-wrote the song, and it was featured on her debut album, *Pink Friday*.

LOVE OF LAUGHTER

Americans love comedies! Since 1995, more than 1,744 funny films have been made in the US, and together they have grossed more than $44.66 billion. Comedies lead the movie market share with 23.49 percent of the audience, followed by adventure movies with 20.0 percent.

SINKING CINEMA SALES

Movie ticket sales have been on the decline, and 2011 was the worst year since 1997. There were 1.28 billion tickets sold, which brought in $10.2 billion in revenue. The most successful movie was *Harry Potter and the Deathly Hallows: Part 2*, which sold 48 million tickets. Warner Bros. made the most movies with 39 films, but Paramount Pictures earned the most with $1.96 billion grossed.

FAN FAVORITE

Super Bowl XLVI became the most watched program of all time on February 5, 2012, when 111.3 million viewers tuned in to watch Eli Manning and the Giants defeat Tom Brady and the Patriots. Advertisers spent a hefty $3.5 million per 30-second commercial to advertise during the game.

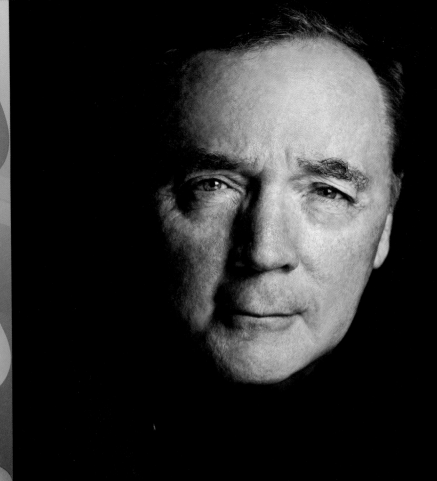

highest-paid author

JAMES PATTERSON

Author James Patterson earned $84 million in 2011. During the year, Patterson released 11 books, including *Witch & Wizard: The Fire*, *Kill Alex Cross*, *Daniel X: Game Over*, *Middle School: The Worst Time of My Life*, *Maximum Ride: Angle*, and *Now You See Her*. Patterson has written more than 70 novels since he retired from advertising in 1985. Of these, 63 have reached the *New York Times* Best Sellers list, which is a list record. Patterson has sold an estimated 220 million books worldwide in the last three years, which is more than any other author during that time.

highest-paid authors
income in 2011,
in millions of US dollars

James Patterson	Danielle Steele	Stephen King	Janet Evanovich	Stephenie Meyer
84	35	28	22	21

highest-paid tv actors

ashton kutcher/hugh laurie

Television mega-stars Ashton Kutcher and Hugh Laurie both pull in $700,000 per episode. In 2011, Kutcher stepped into *Two and a Half Men* as brokenhearted millionaire Walden Schmidt to replace Charlie Sheen. Kutcher's debut was much anticipated, and 27.7 million viewers tuned in to watch his premier episode—the largest audience in the show's nine seasons. Laurie—who began his role as Dr. Gregory House on Fox's medical drama, *House,* in 2004— played a sarcastic but brilliant physician who diagnosed unusual cases. He has won two Golden Globe Awards, and has been nominated for three Emmy Awards for his work on the series. *House*'s final episode aired in May 2012.

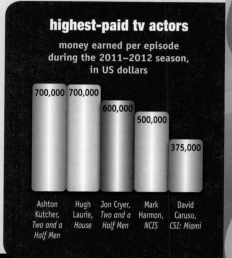

highest-paid tv actors

money earned per episode
during the 2011–2012 season,
in US dollars

Ashton Kutcher, Two and a Half Men	Hugh Laurie, House	Jon Cryer, Two and a Half Men	Mark Harmon, NCIS	David Caruso, CSI: Miami
700,000	700,000	600,000	500,000	375,000

Ashton Kutcher

highest-paid tv actress

Mariska Hargitay

Law & Order: Special Victims Unit actress Mariska Hargitay earns $395,000 per episode for her role as Detective Olivia Benson. Since the NBC crime drama—also known simply as *SVU*—began in 1999, Hargitay has won an Emmy and a Golden Globe for her performance. The series focuses on the 16th precinct of the New York Police Department, and follows the detectives and lawyers from when the crime is committed to how it plays out in the courtroom. The show is a spinoff of the original *Law & Order* series, and was the second in the franchise. *SVU* draws about 8.8 million views each week.

highest-paid tv actresses

money earned per episode during the 2011–2012 season, in US dollars

395,000	375,000	375,000	375,000	375,000
Mariska Hargitay, *Law & Order: SVU*	Marcia Cross, *Desperate House-wives*	Teri Hatcher, *Desperate House-wives*	Felicity Huffman, *Desperate House-wives*	Eva Longoria, *Desperate House-wives*

highest-paid young tv star

ANGUS T. JONES

Nineteen-year-old Angus T. Jones earns a hefty $300,000 per episode for his role as Jake Harper on *Two and a Half Men*. For the 2011–2012 seasons, Jones will earn a total of $7.8 million—plus a $500,000 signing bonus. The sitcom, which also stars Jon Cryer, has been among the top 20 most watched programs since it first aired in 2003. Jones has also appeared in several movies, including *See Spot Run*, *The Rookie*, *Bringing Down the House*, and *George of the Jungle 2*. When he's not in front of a camera, he volunteers for organizations such as Big Brothers Big Sisters and St. Jude's Children's Research Hospital.

highest-paid young tv stars

money earned per episode during the 2011–2012 season, in US dollars

Angus T. Jones, Two and a Half Men	Miranda Cosgrove, iCarly	Selena Gomez, Wizards of Waverly Place	Cole Sprouse, The Suite Life	Dylan Sprouse, The Suite Life
300,000	180,000	30,000	20,000	20,000

tv show with the most emmy awards

Frasier

Frasier—a hugely popular show that ran between 1993 and 2004—picked up 37 Emmy Awards during its 11 seasons. The sitcom focused on the life and family of psychiatrist Dr. Frasier Crane, played by Kelsey Grammer. His costars included David Hyde Pierce, John Mahoney, Peri Gilpin, and Jane Leeves. Some of the 37 awards the series won include Outstanding Comedy Series, Lead Actor in a Comedy Series, Supporting Actor in a Comedy Series, Directing in a Comedy Series, Editing, and Art Direction.

tv shows with the most emmy awards

emmys won

Frasier	Saturday Night Live	The Mary Tyler Moore Show	Cheers	Hill Street Blues
37	32	29	28	26

tv show with the most consecutive emmy awards

THE DAILY SHOW
WITH JON STEWART

The Daily Show with Jon Stewart has won an Emmy Award for Outstanding Variety, Music or Comedy Special for nine consecutive seasons between 2003 and 2011. In total, the show has received 23 Emmy nominations, and has won 16 of them. Although it is considered a fake news show, the program often uses actual recent news stories and delivers them with a funny or sarcastic spin. The show began in 1996, and it is the longest-running program on Comedy Central. *The Daily Show* was hosted by Craig Kilborn until 1998, when Kilborn was replaced by Stewart.

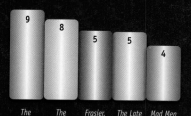

tv shows with the most consecutive emmy awards
emmys won

Show	Emmys
The Daily Show with Jon Stewart, 2003–2011	9
The Amazing Race, 2003–2009	8
Frasier, 1994–1998	5
The Late Show with David Letterman, 1998–2002	5
Mad Men 2008–2011	4

most popular scripted tv show

NCIS

Crime drama *NCIS* averages more than 19 million viewers each week. The show, which stands for Naval Criminal Investigation Service, focuses on a team of agents that investigate crimes involving the Navy and Marine Corps. *NCIS* premiered in 2003 and stars Mark Harmon (Supervisory Special Agent Leroy Jethro Gibbs), Michael Weatherly (Special Agent Anthony DiNozzo), Sean Murray (Special Agent Tim McGee), and Cote De Pablo (Special Agent Ziva David). The show has been nominated for several Emmys and People's Choice awards, and won seven ASCAP Awards.

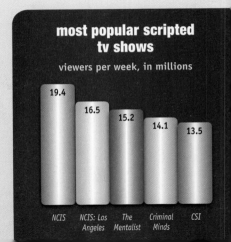

most popular scripted tv shows

viewers per week, in millions

NCIS	NCIS: Los Angeles	The Mentalist	Criminal Minds	CSI
19.4	16.5	15.2	14.1	13.5

most popular reality tv show

AMERICAN IDOL

More than 8 percent of the TV-viewing audience tuned in during the 2011 season to watch the tenth installment of *American Idol*. During this ultimate reality singing contest, viewers watched Scotty McCreery defeat Lauren Alaina after fans cast nearly 122 million votes. McCreery and Alaina are the two youngest finalists in the show's history. McCreery bested 35 other contestants and braved comments from judges Steven Tyler, Jennifer Lopez, and Randy Jackson. *American Idol* is one of just three television shows that have been rated number one for six consecutive seasons.

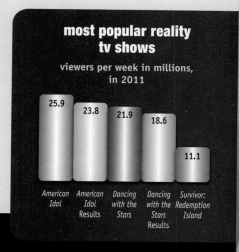

most popular reality tv shows

viewers per week in millions, in 2011

American Idol	American Idol Results	Dancing with the Stars	Dancing with the Stars Results	Survivor: Redemption Island
25.9	23.8	21.9	18.6	11.1

Scotty McCreery

highest-paid director/producer

TYLER PERRY

Movie and TV producer Tyler Perry raked in $130 million in 2011. On the small screen, Perry produces *House of Payne* and *Meet the Browns*—the highest-rated and second-highest-rated first-run syndicated cable shows of all time. On the silver screen, Perry released *Madea's Big Happy Family*, the fifth installment of the Madea franchise. The films have grossed a combined $309 million worldwide. Perry also opened his own studio in Atlanta that includes five soundstages, a post-production facility, a backlot, and a 400-seat theater.

highest-paid directors/producers

income in 2011, in millions of US dollars

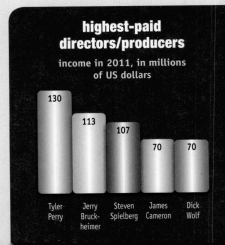

Tyler Perry	Jerry Bruckheimer	Steven Spielberg	James Cameron	Dick Wolf
130	113	107	70	70

BEN-HUR, TITANIC & THE LORD OF THE RINGS: THE RETURN OF THE KING

The only three films in Hollywood history to win 11 Academy Awards are *Ben-Hur*, *Titanic*, and *The Lord of the Rings: The Return of the King*. Some of the Oscar wins for *Ben-Hur*—a biblical epic based on an 1880 novel by General Lew Wallace—include Best Actor (Charlton Heston) and Director (William Wyler). Some of *Titanic*'s Oscars include Best Cinematography, Visual Effects, and Costume Design. *The Lord of the Rings: The Return of the King* is the final film in the epic trilogy based on the works of J. R. R. Tolkien. With 11 awards, it is the most successful movie in Academy Awards history because it won every category in which it was nominated. Some of these wins include Best Picture, Director (Peter Jackson), and Costume Design.

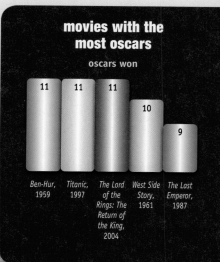

movies with the most oscars

oscars won

Ben-Hur, 1959	Titanic, 1997	The Lord of the Rings: The Return of the King, 2004	West Side Story, 1961	The Last Emperor, 1987
11	11	11	10	9

Presenters and the cast of *The Lord of the Rings* (Peter Jackson in front)

actress with the most oscar nominations
MERYL STREEP

Meryl Streep is the most nominated actress in the history of the Academy Awards with 17 chances to win a statue. Her first nomination came in 1979 for *The Deer Hunter*, and was followed by *Kramer vs. Kramer* (1980), *The French Lieutenant's Woman* (1981), *Sophie's Choice* (1982), *Silkwood* (1983), *Out of Africa* (1985), *Ironweed* (1987), *A Cry in the Dark* (1988), *Postcards From the Edge* (1990), *The Bridges of Madison County* (1995), *One True Thing* (1998), *Music of the Heart* (1999), *Adaptation* (2002), *The Devil Wears Prada* (2006), *Doubt* (2008), *Julie and Julia* (2009), and *The Iron Lady* (2012). Streep won her first Academy Award for *Kramer vs. Kramer*, her second for *Sophie's Choice*, and a third for *The Iron Lady*.

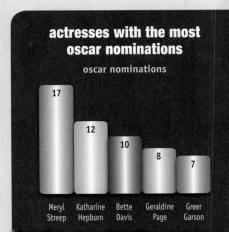

actresses with the most oscar nominations
oscar nominations

Meryl Streep	Katharine Hepburn	Bette Davis	Geraldine Page	Greer Garson
17	12	10	8	7

actor with the most oscar nominations

Jack NICHOLSON

Jack Nicholson has been nominated for a record 12 Oscars during his distinguished career. He is one of only three men to have been nominated for an acting Academy Award at least once every decade for five decades. He was nominated for eight Best Actor awards for his roles in *Five Easy Pieces* (1970), *The Last Detail* (1973), *Chinatown* (1974), *One Flew Over the Cuckoo's Nest* (1975), *Prizzi's Honor* (1985), *Ironweed* (1987), *As Good as It Gets* (1997), and *About Schmidt* (2002). He was nominated for Best Supporting Actor for *Easy Rider* (1969), *Reds* (1981), *Terms of Endearment* (1983), and *A Few Good Men* (1992). Nicholson picked up statues for *One Flew Over the Cuckoo's Nest*, *Terms of Endearment*, and *As Good as It Gets*.

actors with the most oscar nominations

oscar nominations

Jack Nicholson	Laurence Olivier	Paul Newman	Spencer Tracy	Al Pacino
12	10	9	9	8

actor with the most mtv movie awards

JIM carrey

Jim Carrey has won 11 MTV Movie Awards since the television station began awarding them in 1992. He has won the award for Best Comedic Performance five times, for his roles in *Dumb & Dumber* (1995), *Ace Ventura II: When Nature Calls* (1996), *The Cable Guy* (1997), *Liar Liar* (1998), and *Yes Man* (2009). Carrey won the award for Best Male Performance twice, for *Ace Ventura II: When Nature Calls* and *The Truman Show* (1999). He also won awards for Best Kiss for *Dumb & Dumber*, Best Villain for *The Cable Guy*, and the MTV Generation Award in 2006.

actors with the most mtv movie awards

awards won

Jim Carrey	Robert Pattinson	Mike Myers	Adam Sandler	Will Smith
11	9	7	6	5

actress with the most mtv movie awards
Kristen Stewart

Kristen Stewart, who rose to fame playing Bella Swan in the Twilight saga, has won seven MTV Movie Awards for her role. She picked up her first two awards—Best Female Performance and Best Kiss—in 2009 for *Twilight*. She shared the Best Kiss award with co-star Robert Pattinson. A year later, she picked up the same two awards for *New Moon*. In 2011, Stewart nabbed the same two again for *Eclipse*. Stewart's most recent award win came in 2012, when she once again shared the Best Kiss award with Robert Pattinson for the 2011 Twilight film, *Breaking Dawn: Part One*.

actresses with the most mtv movie awards
awards won

Kristen Stewart	Alicia Silver-stone	Uma Thurman	Drew Barrymore	Kirsten Dunst
7	4	4	3	3

actress with the highest average box-office gross

emma watson

Emma Watson, who is best known for her role as Hermione Granger in the Harry Potter franchise, has an average of $245.5 million per picture. The franchise, which included eight movies between 2001 and 2011, grossed more than $7.7 billion worldwide. Some of Watson's other roles include Lucy in *My Week with Marilyn* (2011), and the voice of Princess Pea in *The Tale of Despereaux*. The actress was born in Paris, France, and got her big break when she was cast in the first Potter film when she was 9. She has since won three Teen Choice Awards and one People's Choice Award for her work on the franchise.

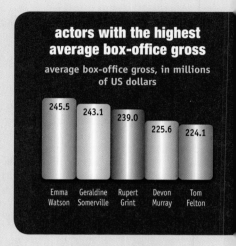

actors with the highest average box-office gross

average box-office gross, in millions of US dollars

Emma Watson	Geraldine Somerville	Rupert Grint	Devon Murray	Tom Felton
245.5	243.1	239.0	225.6	224.1

actor with the highest career box-office gross

FranK WeLKer

Frank Welker's movies have a combined total gross of $6.42 billion. Although movie fans might not recognize Welker's name or face, they would probably recognize many of his voices. Welker is a voice actor, and has worked on more than 90 movies in the last 25 years. Some of his most famous voices include Megatron, Curious George, and Scooby-Doo. Welker's most profitable movies include *How the Grinch Stole Christmas*, *Godzilla*, and *101 Dalmatians*.

actors with the highest career box-office gross

total gross, in billions of US dollars*

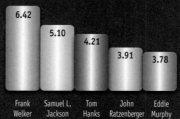

Frank Welker	Samuel L. Jackson	Tom Hanks	John Ratzenberger	Eddie Murphy
6.42	5.10	4.21	3.91	3.78

*As of January 2012

top-grossing animated movie

TOY STORY 3

With earnings of more than $1.06 billion worldwide, *Toy Story 3* has easily become the highest-grossing animated movie in history. It is also the seventh-highest-grossing movie ever. The Disney-Pixar movie opened on June 18, 2010, and earned $110 million during its first three days in theaters. The plot of the third installment of the Toy Story franchise follows Woody as he leads the other toys out of a day-care center where they were mistakenly delivered. The toys' famous voices included Tom Hanks (Woody), Tim Allen (Buzz), Joan Cusack (Jessie), and John Ratzenberger (Hamm).

top-grossing animated movies

total worldwide gross, in US dollars

Toy Story 3	The Lion King	Shrek 2	Ice Age: Dawn of the Dinosaurs	Finding Nemo
1.06B	952.80M	919.80M	886.96M	867.89M

movie with the most successful opening weekend

HARRY POTTER AND THE DEATHLY HALLOWS: PART 2

When *Harry Potter and the Deathly Hallows: Part 2* debuted on July 15, 2011, the eighth installment of the wizard phenomenon hauled in $169.1 million over three days. The movie also claimed the record for the biggest opening day of all time, with a gross of $92 million. The final film in the Harry Potter series starred Daniel Radcliffe as Harry, Emma Watson as Hermione, and Rupert Grint as Ron. Together they search for Lord Voldemort's Horcruxes in an effort to finally defeat him. Combined, the Harry Potter movies have earned more than $7 billion worldwide.

movies with the most successful opening weekends

weekend earnings, in millions of US dollars

169.1	Harry Potter and the Deathly Hallows: Part 2, 7/15/11
158.4	The Dark Knight, 7/18/08
152.5	The Hunger Games, 3/23/12
151.2	Spider-Man 3, 5/4/07
142.8	The Twilight Saga: New Moon, 11/20/09

top-grossing movie
avaTar

Avatar, James Cameron's science-fiction epic, was released in December 2009 and grossed more than $2.78 billion worldwide in less than two months. Starring Sigourney Weaver, Sam Worthington, and Zoe Saldana, *Avatar* cost more than $230 million to make. Cameron began working on the film in 1994, and it was eventually filmed in 3-D, with special cameras made just for the movie. Due to *Avatar*'s overwhelming success, Cameron is already planning two sequels.

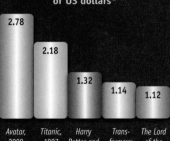

top-grossing movies
total worldwide gross, in billions of US dollars*

2.78	2.18	1.32	1.14	1.12
Avatar, 2009	Titanic, 1997	Harry Potter and the Deathly Hallows: Part 2, 2011	Trans-formers: Dark of the Moon, 2011	The Lord of the Rings: The Return of the King, 2003

*As of May 15, 2012

most successful movie franchise

Harry Potter

The first seven movies in the Harry Potter franchise have collectively earned $7.70 billion. The series, which began in November 2001, is based on the bestselling books by J. K. Rowling. They chronicle the adventures of a young wizard—Harry Potter—as he grows up and learns of the great power he possesses. The highest-grossing movie in the franchise is the last one—*Harry Potter and the Deathly Hallows: Part 2*—which earned $1.3 billion worldwide. The leads of the movie, including Daniel Radcliffe, Rupert Grint, and Emma Watson, have become some of the highest-paid young stars in Hollywood.

most successful movie franchises

total worldwide gross, in billions of US dollars

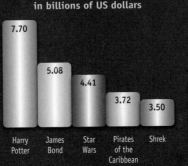

Harry Potter	James Bond	Star Wars	Pirates of the Caribbean	Shrek
7.70	5.08	4.41	3.72	3.50

*As of March 3, 2012

top-earning actor

LEONARDO DiCAPRIO

Leonardo DiCaprio raked in $77 million during 2011, mostly due to the huge success of his two 2010 films—*Inception* and *Shutter Island*. *Inception* was the sixth-highest-grossing movie in 2010 with worldwide box office receipts of $832.6 million. In this sci-fi thriller, DiCaprio played thief Dom Cobb. In *Shutter Island*—which grossed around $296 million worldwide— DiCaprio played Teddy Daniels, a US Marshal searching for a missing woman. DiCaprio is a known bankable star, with an average box office gross of $78.5 million. His most profitable and well-known role was in 1997 when he starred as Jack Dawson in *Titanic*. In April 2012, *Titanic* was back on the silver screen in 3-D, and millions of moviegoers flocked to see it.

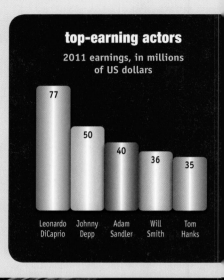

top-earning actors

2011 earnings, in millions of US dollars

Leonardo DiCaprio	Johnny Depp	Adam Sandler	Will Smith	Tom Hanks
77	50	40	36	35

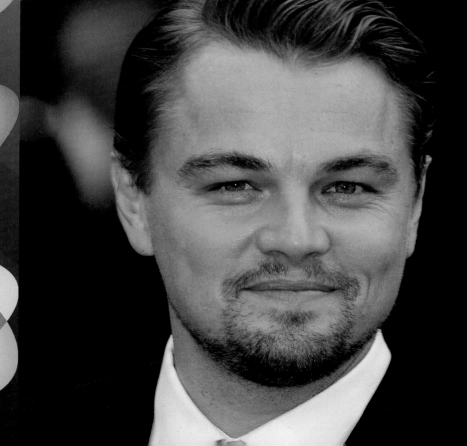

Angelina Jolie

top-earning actresses

ANGELINA JOLIE
& SARAH JESSICA PARKER

Blockbuster stars Angelina Jolie and Sarah Jessica Parker each earned $30 million in 2011. Jolie voiced the character Master Tigress in *Kung Fu Panda 2*, which earned $665 million worldwide at the box office. She also wrote and directed the 2011 film *In the Land of Blood and Honey*. It was well received, and the movie received a Golden Globe nomination for Best Foreign Language Film. Parker's income came mostly from reprising her role as Carrie Bradshaw in *Sex and the City 2*. The movie grossed $294 million worldwide and was based on the popular TV series of the same name, which ran on HBO from 1998–2004.

top-earning actresses

2011 earnings, in millions of US dollars

Angelina Jolie	Sarah Jessica Parker	Jennifer Aniston	Reese Witherspoon	Kristen Stewart
30	30	28	28	20

highest animated-movie budget

TANGLED

Walt Disney Animation Studios budgeted $260 million for its latest fairy-tale remake, *Tangled*—and the big bucks paid off. *Tangled* more than doubled that figure with a worldwide gross of $586 million. Animators used computer-generated imagery (CGI) to create the film, but it was also combined with hand-drawn images to resemble classic fairy-tale films. Released in 2010, *Tangled* follows the journey of Rapunzel, from her tower deep in the forest to a reunion with her long-lost family. Mandy Moore, Zachary Levi, and Donna Murphy lent their voices to the main characters.

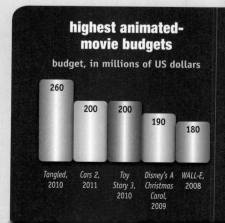

highest animated-movie budgets

budget, in millions of US dollars

260	200	200	190	180
Tangled, 2010	Cars 2, 2011	Toy Story 3, 2010	Disney's A Christmas Carol, 2009	WALL-E, 2008

highest movie budget

PIRATES OF THE CARIBBEAN: AT WORLD'S END

With a budget of $300 million, the creators of *Pirates of the Caribbean: At World's End* spent the most money in movie history. And all of that money seems to have paid off. The third installment of the Pirates series opened in May 2007 and has since earned more than $961 million worldwide. It is the fifth-highest-grossing movie worldwide, and had the fourth-highest domestic gross in 2007. The Jerry Bruckheimer blockbuster starred Johnny Depp as Captain Jack Sparrow, Orlando Bloom as Will Turner, and Keira Knightley as Elizabeth Swann.

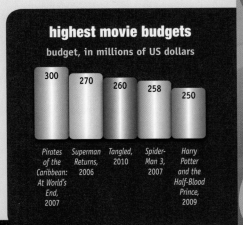

highest movie budgets

budget, in millions of US dollars

300	270	260	258	250
Pirates of the Caribbean: At World's End, 2007	Superman Returns, 2006	Tangled, 2010	Spider-Man 3, 2007	Harry Potter and the Half-Blood Prince, 2009

Harry Potter and the Deathly Hallows: Part 2

On July 15, 2011, fans rushed to theaters to see *Harry Potter and the Deathly Hallows: Part 2*, spending $91 million in a single day. It was released in 4,375 theaters and earned an average of $20,816 per location. The final film in the wizard franchise went on to earn $1.3 billion worldwide—making it the third-highest-grossing movie of all time. It also holds the record for the film to earn $150 million in the shortest amount of time. *Harry Potter and the Deathly Hallows: Part 2* was nominated for three Academy Awards in 2011—Art Direction, Visual Effects, and Makeup.

movies that earned the most in a single day

box-office earnings, in millions of US dollars

Harry Potter and the Deathly Hallows: Part 2, 7/15/11	91.0
The Twilight Saga: New Moon, 11/20/09	72.7
The Twilight Saga: Breaking Dawn: Part 1, 11/18/11	71.6
The Twilight Saga: Eclipse, 6/30/10	68.5
The Dark Knight, 7/18/08	67.1

top-selling dvd

Harry Potter and the Deathly Hallows: Part 1

DVD copies of *Harry Potter and the Deathly Hallows: Part 1* flew off the shelves in 2011, selling more than 7 million copies. The DVD was released on April 15, 2011, and has earned more than $85.9 million since then. The movie debuted in theaters in November 2010 and earned $956 million worldwide. It was the third-highest-grossing movie of the franchise. The adventure movie, based on the bestselling books of J. K. Rowling, follows Harry, Ron, and Hermione on their quest to find and destroy the five remaining horcruxes.

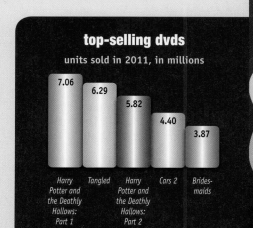

top-selling dvds

units sold in 2011, in millions

Harry Potter and the Deathly Hallows: Part 1	Tangled	Harry Potter and the Deathly Hallows: Part 2	Cars 2	Brides-maids
7.06	6.29	5.82	4.40	3.87

bestselling movie soundtrack

THE BODYGUARD

The soundtrack of *The Bodyguard* has sold more than 17 million copies since it was released in November 1992. The movie starred Kevin Costner as a former FBI agent in charge of a pop singer, played by Whitney Houston. Houston produced the soundtrack, along with Clive Davis, and it features three of Houston's biggest hits—"I Will Always Love You," "I Have Nothing," and "I'm Every Woman." The album picked up a Grammy for Album of the Year and reached number one on music charts worldwide, including Australia, Canada, France, Germany, and Japan.

bestselling movie soundtracks

units sold, in millions

The Bodyguard	Saturday Night Fever	Purple Rain	Forrest Gump	Titanic
17	15	13	12	11

THE BEATLES

The Beatles have sold 177 million copies of their albums in the United States since their first official recording session in September 1962. In the two years that followed, they had 26 Top 40 singles. John Lennon, Paul McCartney, George Harrison, and Ringo Starr made up the "Fab Four," as the Beatles were known. Together they recorded many albums that are now considered rock masterpieces, such as *Rubber Soul*, *Sgt. Pepper's Lonely Hearts Club Band*, and *The Beatles.* The group broke up in 1969. In 2001, however, their newly released greatest hits album—*The Beatles 1*—reached the top of the charts. One of their best-known songs—"Yesterday"—is the most recorded song in history, with about 2,500 different artists recording their own versions.

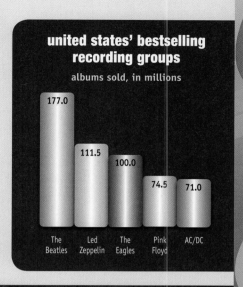

united states' bestselling recording groups

albums sold, in millions

The Beatles	Led Zeppelin	The Eagles	Pink Floyd	AC/DC
177.0	111.5	100.0	74.5	71.0

top-selling recording artist

adele

English singer-songwriter Adele sold more than 6.7 million albums in 2011. She has released two albums—*19* and *21*—since her career began in 2006. The singer has picked up some prestigious awards during her short career. In 2008, she was nominated for four Grammys and won two—Best New Artist and Best Female Pop Vocal Performance. In 2011, she won six Grammys and became just the second woman in history to accomplish this in one evening (after Beyoncé in 2009). Some of Adele's wins included Song of the Year, Album of the Year, and Record of the Year.

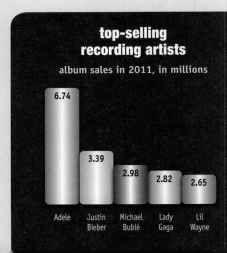

top-selling recording artists

album sales in 2011, in millions

Adele	Justin Bieber	Michael Bublé	Lady Gaga	Lil Wayne
6.74	3.39	2.98	2.82	2.65

most downloaded song

"ROLLING IN THE DEEP"

The most downloaded song in America during 2011 was "Rolling in the Deep" by Adele, with more than 5.8 million purchases. That's enough for every person living in the state of Maryland to own a copy! The song was co-written by Adele, and was released in November 2010 from her *21* album. Adele embarked on her Adele Live tour in May 2011 to promote *21*, but had to cut it short that November due to throat surgery. She made her dramatic comeback at the 2012 Grammy Awards, where she performed "Rolling in the Deep" to much fanfare.

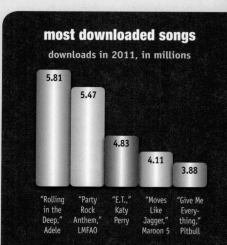

most downloaded songs

downloads in 2011, in millions

5.81	5.47	4.83	4.11	3.88
"Rolling in the Deep," Adele	"Party Rock Anthem," LMFAO	"E.T.," Katy Perry	"Moves Like Jagger," Maroon 5	"Give Me Every-thing," Pitbull

most downloaded recording artist

KATY PERRY

More than 15 million of Katy Perry's singles were downloaded in 2011. "E.T." was Perry's biggest seller and the year's third most-downloaded song with 4.8 million copies sold. Perry's other recent hits include "California Gurls," "Last Friday Night (T.G.I.F.)," "Firework," and "The One That Got Away." At the 2011 American Music Awards, Perry received a special achievement award for becoming the first female pop artist to have five number-one hits from a single album—*Teenage Dream*. Perry has also won eight People's Choice Awards, four Teen Choice Awards, and two Billboard Music Awards.

most downloaded recording artists

songs downloaded in 2011, in millions

15.18	14.24	13.91	13.58	12.76
Katy Perry	Adele	Rihanna	*Glee* Cast	Lady Gaga

bestselling digital artist of all time

rihanna

Between 2004 and 2011, Rihanna sold more than 47.5 million songs online. Her six studio albums—*Music of the Sun* (2005), *A Girl Like Me* (2006), *Good Girl Gone Bad* (2007), *Rated R* (2009), *Loud* (2010), and *Talk That Talk* (2011)— feature dozens of hits. Some of her most popular songs include "We Found Love," "Disturbia," "Don't Stop the Music," "Only Girl (in the World)," and "Umbrella." She has sold more than 20 million albums and won many awards, including 4 Grammy Awards, 5 American Music Awards, and 18 Billboard Music Awards.

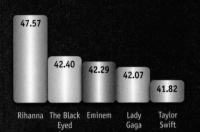

bestselling digital artists of all time

total units sold, in millions

Rihanna	The Black Eyed Peas	Eminem	Lady Gaga	Taylor Swift
47.57	42.40	42.29	42.07	41.82

bestselling digital song of all time

"I GOTTA FEELING"

The Black Eyed Peas' mega dance hit "I Gotta Feeling" is the bestselling digital song of all time with more than 7.6 million downloads. The song, which was released in May 2009, is from The Black Eyed Peas' fifth studio album, *The E.N.D.* "I Gotta Feeling" won a Grammy Award for Best Pop Performance by a Duo or Group, and was nominated for Song of the Year at the World Music Awards. The song was number one on the Billboard Hot 100 chart for 12 straight weeks and also topped music charts in 25 other countries. The members of the group are will.i.am, apl.de.ap, Taboo, and Fergie.

bestselling digital songs of all time
units sold, in millions

"I Gotta Feeling," The Black Eyed Peas	"Poker Face," Lady Gaga	"Just Dance," Lady Gaga	"Boom Boom Pow," The Black Eyed Peas	"Low," Flo Rida
7.68	6.52	6.45	6.26	6.15

top-earning hip-hop artist

JaY-Z

Rapper Jay-Z earned $37 million in 2011. Although he did not release his own album in 2011, Jay-Z collaborated with several successful artists including Eminem, Kanye West, U2, Rihanna, and M.I.A. Jay-Z also published his memoir, *Decoded*, in 2010. In addition to his book and music, Jay-Z is a successful entrepreneur. He is part owner of the Brooklyn Nets basketball team and owns a chain of sports restaurants located in airports across the country.

top-earning hip-hop artists
earnings in 2011, in millions of US dollars

Jay-Z	Will Smith	Sean (Diddy) Combs	Kanye West	Lil Wayne
37	36	35	16	15

bestselling album

21

Adele dominated album sales in 2011, selling more than 5.8 million copies of *21*. That's more than the year's next two top sellers combined! The album, which was named for Adele's age at the time of production, was released in January 2011. The first three singles released from the album include "Rolling in the Deep," "Someone Like You," and "Set Fire to the Rain." All three reached the top of the charts worldwide. *21* won three American Music Awards including Favorite Pop/Rock Album, Favorite Female Artist, and Adult Contemporary Artist: Favorite Artist.

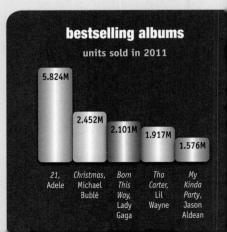

bestselling albums

units sold in 2011

5.824M	2.452M	2.101M	1.917M	1.576M
21, Adele	*Christmas,* Michael Bublé	*Born This Way,* Lady Gaga	*Tha Carter,* Lil Wayne	*My Kinda Party,* Jason Aldean

bestselling digital album of all time

21

21—the second studio album from Adele—has become the most downloaded album of all time, with 1.8 million copies sold. The record has also sold more than 17 million hard copies worldwide, with about half of those sales in the United States. 21's lead single, "Rolling in the Deep," has sold more than 5.75 million digital copies worldwide. The single was first released in November 2010 and has reached number one on the charts in six countries, including the United States. Adele, a singer and songwriter from England, is known for her unique blend of folk, R&B, country, and blues styles.

bestselling digital albums of all time

total digital albums sold

1.8M	1.10M	1.08M	1.01M	877,000
21, Adele	Sigh No More, Mumford & Sons	Recovery, Eminem	The Fame, Lady Gaga	Born This Way, Lady Gaga

top-earning male singer

ELTON JOHN

Vocal legend Sir Elton John earned $100 million in 2011. Between 2010 and 2011, he performed 102 live shows to promote his latest album, *The Union*. The tour earned $204 million worldwide. In September 2011, John began a three-year run at Caesar's Palace in Las Vegas performing a show called "The Million Dollar Piano." A month later, he played the 3,000th concert of his career there. Elton John has sold more than 250 million records and released 30 studio albums in his thirty-year career. He was inducted into the Rock and Roll Hall of Fame in 1994.

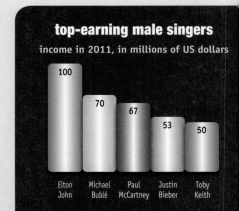

top-earning male singers
income in 2011, in millions of US dollars

Elton John	Michael Bublé	Paul McCartney	Justin Bieber	Toby Keith
100	70	67	53	50

top-earning female singer
LaDY GaGa

The eccentric Lady Gaga brought in $90 million and topped *Forbes*'s Most Powerful Celebrity list in 2011. In May 2011, her second studio album, *Born This Way*, sold more than 1.1 million copies on the first day it was released. Featuring hits like the title track, "You and I," and "The Edge of Glory," the album topped the charts in the United States and 20 other countries. In July 2011, Gaga became the first Twitter user to top 12 million followers. Her Facebook page has more than 36 million fans. In November that year, the television special *A Very Gaga Thanksgiving* scored 5.7 million viewers.

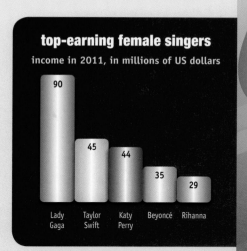

top-earning female singers

income in 2011, in millions of US dollars

Lady Gaga	Taylor Swift	Katy Perry	Beyoncé	Rihanna
90	45	44	35	29

most played song

"ROLLING IN THE DEEP"

"Rolling in the Deep" by Adele was played on the radio approximately 658,000 times in 2011. The song's blend of rock, pop, and soul appeals to a wide range of listeners. It is one of the most successful "crossover" songs in Billboard history, meaning that it is played on a wide variety of different radio stations—from rock and pop to Latin and dance. The song's video was also well received, earning seven MTV Video Awards. It won three, including Best Editing, Best Cinematography, and Best Art Direction.

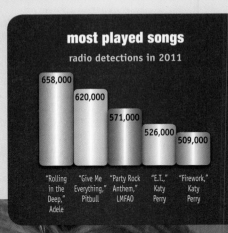

most played songs
radio detections in 2011

"Rolling in the Deep," Adele	"Give Me Everything," Pitbull	"Party Rock Anthem," LMFAO	"E.T.," Katy Perry	"Firework," Katy Perry
658,000	620,000	571,000	526,000	509,000

musician with the most mtv video music awards

MADONNA

Madonna has won 20 MTV Video Music Awards since the ceremony was first held in 1984. She has won four Cinematography awards, three Female Video awards, three Directing awards, two Editing awards, and two Art Direction awards. She also picked up single awards for Video of the Year, Choreography, Special Effects, and Long Form Video, as well as a Viewer's Choice and a Video Vanguard Award. Madonna's award-winning videos include "Papa Don't Preach," "Like a Prayer," "Express Yourself," "Vogue," "Rain," "Take a Bow," "Ray of Light," and "Beautiful Stranger."

musicians with the most mtv video music awards

awards won

Madonna	Peter Gabriel	Lady Gaga	R.E.M.	Eminem
20	13	13	12	11

top-earning tour

U2

U2 rocked 2011 with a concert tour that grossed more than $293 million. They sold out all of their 44 shows, and played in front of almost 2.9 million fans. This was the third leg of their U2 360° tour, which began in 2009. Concerts took place in South America and South Africa, as well as in North America, where the group made up some dates that were previously canceled due to frontman Bono's back injury. Over its three-year run, the U2 360° tour earned $736 million and was enjoyed by 7.2 million fans. This set a record for both income and attendance for a single concert tour.

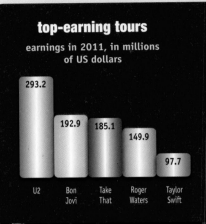

top-earning tours

earnings in 2011, in millions of US dollars

U2	Bon Jovi	Take That	Roger Waters	Taylor Swift
293.2	192.9	185.1	149.9	97.7

act with the most country music awards

GEORGE STRAIT

George Strait has won a whopping 22 Country Music Awards and has been nicknamed the "King of Country" for all of his accomplishments in the business. He won his first CMA award in 1985, and his most recent in 2008. In addition to his many awards, Strait holds the record for the most number one hits on the Billboard Hot Country Songs with 44. He also has 38 hit albums, including 12 multiplatinum and 22 platinum records. He was inducted into the Country Music Hall of Fame in 2006.

acts with the most country music awards

awards won

George Strait	Brooks & Dunn	Vince Gill	Alan Jackson	Brad Paisley
22	19	18	16	14

longest-running broadway show

THE PHANTOM OF THE OPERA

The Phantom of the Opera has been performed more than 9,977 times since it opened in January 1988. The show tells the story of a disfigured musical genius who terrorizes the performers of the Paris Opera House. More than 100 million people have seen a performance in 144 cities and 27 countries. The show won seven Tony Awards its opening year, including Best Musical. The musical drama is performed at the Majestic Theater.

longest-running broadway shows
total performances*

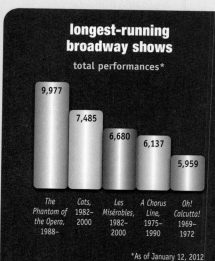

The Phantom of the Opera, 1988–	Cats, 1982–2000	Les Misérables, 1982–2000	A Chorus Line, 1975–1990	Oh! Calcutta! 1969–1972
9,977	7,485	6,680	6,137	5,959

*As of January 12, 2012

musical with the most tony awards

THE PRODUCERS

In March 2001, *The Producers* took home 12 of its record-breaking 15 Tony Award nominations. The Broadway smash won awards for Musical, Original Score, Book, Direction of a Musical, Choreography, Orchestration, Scenic Design, Costume Design, Lighting Design, Actor in a Musical, Featured Actor in a Musical, and Actress in a Musical. *The Producers*, which originally starred Nathan Lane and Matthew Broderick, is a stage adaptation of Mel Brooks's 1968 movie. Brooks wrote the lyrics and music for 16 new songs for the stage version.

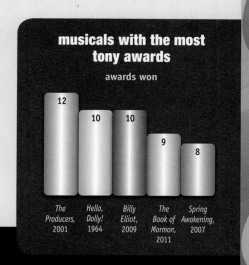

musicals with the most tony awards

awards won

The Producers, 2001	Hello, Dolly! 1964	Billy Elliot, 2009	The Book of Mormon, 2011	Spring Awakening, 2007
12	10	10	9	8

Nature records

natural formations ◐ animals ◐ weather
plants ◐ disasters ◐ environment

clean-up crew

Tasmanian devils are the largest meat-eating marsupials in the world. They are only found on the island of Tasmania in Australia. They were named "devils" because of the growling and shrieking noises they make when feeding on carcasses. They are known as the "vacuum cleaners of the forest" because they eat whatever dead things they come across.

LONG LIMBS

The Arctic Lion's Mane
jellyfish are truly gigantic.
The largest one ever seen
measured more than 7 feet
(2.1 m) across and had
tentacles that stretched
120 feet (36.5 m) long.
Jellyfish have no brain,
blood, bones, or heart.
They are made up of about
95 percent water, but they
have deadly venom in their
tentacles that can paralyze
victims.

eN-LIGHTNING WeaTHeR

Lightning is very common—about 100 bolts strike the earth's surface every second. And each of those bolts can contain up to 1 billion volts of electricity. A single flash can heat the air around it to a temperature five times hotter than the surface of the sun. It's that quick heating of air that produces the rumble of thunder.

DRY AND TASTY

Welwitschia mirabilis—a plant that only grows in Namibia—has just two leaves and a stem. But this sturdy desert plant can live for 1,500 years and can survive up to five years without any water. It can grow up to 6.5 feet (2 m) wide and 26 feet (8 m) high. Some Namibians eat it raw, or baked in ashes.

Deep Discovery

In June 2011, a species of "devil worms" was discovered 2.2 miles (3.6 km) below Earth's surface, making it the deepest-dwelling creature ever. The worms were found in a South African mine, and evidence indicates that this species has been there for about 12,000 years. They've adapted to withstand the intense pressure and heat of the surrounding soil.

One Gusty Month

The busiest calendar month for tornadoes in the United States occurred in March 2003. During those 31 days, some 543 tornadoes swept through the country. Affected states included Arkansas, Illinois, Kansas, Kentucky, Oklahoma, Missouri, Tennessee, and Texas.

Earthly Extremes

The Ring of Fire is a 25,000-mile (40,234 km) stretch of land and water that surrounds the Pacific Ocean from Australia to eastern Asia to western North America to the western side of South America. About 75 percent of the world's active volcanoes are located here, and 90 percent of all earthquakes occur here. There are about 1,500 active volcanoes worldwide.

largest diamond

GOLDEN JUBILEE

The Golden Jubilee is the world's largest faceted diamond, with a weight of 545.67 carats. This gigantic gem got its name when it was presented to the king of Thailand in 1997 for the Golden Jubilee—or 50th anniversary celebration—of his reign. The diamond weighed 755.5 carats when it was discovered in a South African mine in 1986. Once it was cut, the diamond featured 148 perfectly symmetrical facets. The process took almost a year because of the diamond's size and multiple tension points. The diamond is on display at the Royal Museum of Bangkok in Thailand.

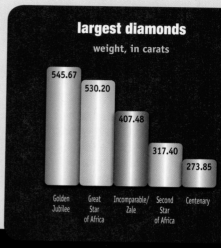

largest diamonds

weight, in carats

Golden Jubilee	Great Star of Africa	Incomparable/ Zale	Second Star of Africa	Centenary
545.67	530.20	407.48	317.40	273.85

tallest mountain

MOUNT everest

Mount Everest's tallest peak towers 29,035 feet (8,850 m) into the air, and it is the highest point on Earth. This peak is an unbelievable 5.5 miles (8.8 km) above sea level. Mount Everest is located in the Himalayas, on the border between Nepal and Tibet. The mountain got its official name from surveyor Sir George Everest. In 1953, Sir Edmund Hillary and Tenzing Norgay were the first people to reach the peak. In 2008, the Olympic torch was carried up to the top of the mountain on its way to the games in Beijing.

tallest mountains

highest point, in feet (meters)

Mount Everest, Asia	K2, Asia	Kangchen-junga, Asia	Lhotse, Asia	Makalu, Asia
29,035 (8,850)	28,250 (8,611)	28,169 (8,586)	27,940 (8,516)	27,766 (8,463)

largest lake

caspian sea

This giant inland body of salt water stretches for almost 750 miles (1,207 km) from north to south, with an average width of about 200 miles (322 km). Altogether, it covers 143,200 square miles (370,901 sq km). The Caspian Sea is located east of the Caucasus Mountains in central Asia. It is bordered by Iran, Russia, Kazakhstan, Azerbaijan, and Turkmenistan. The Caspian Sea has an average depth of about 550 feet (170 m). It is an important fishing resource, with species including sturgeon, salmon, perch, herring, and carp. Other animals living in the Caspian Sea include porpoises, seals, and tortoises. The sea is estimated to be 30 million years old and became landlocked 5.5 million years ago.

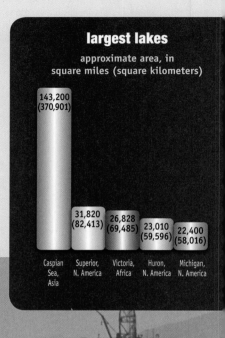

largest lakes

approximate area, in
square miles (square kilometers)

Caspian Sea, Asia	Superior, N. America	Victoria, Africa	Huron, N. America	Michigan, N. America
143,200 (370,901)	31,820 (82,413)	26,828 (69,485)	23,010 (59,596)	22,400 (58,016)

largest desert

saнara

Located in northern Africa, the Sahara Desert covers approximately 3.5 million square miles (9.1 million sq km). It stretches for 5,200 miles (8,372 km) through the countries of Morocco, Algeria, Tunisia, Libya, Egypt, Mauritania, Mali, Niger, Chad, and Sudan. The Sahara gets very little rainfall—less than 8 inches (20 cm) per year. Even with its harsh environment, some 2.5 million people—mostly nomads—call the Sahara home. Date palms and acacias grow near oases. Some of the animals that live in the Sahara include gazelles, antelopes, jackals, foxes, and badgers.

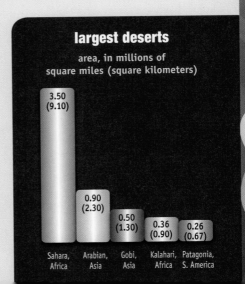

largest deserts

area, in millions of square miles (square kilometers)

Desert	Area
Sahara, Africa	3.50 (9.10)
Arabian, Asia	0.90 (2.30)
Gobi, Asia	0.50 (1.30)
Kalahari, Africa	0.36 (0.90)
Patagonia, S. America	0.26 (0.67)

longest river

NILE

The Nile River in Africa stretches 4,145 miles (6,671 km) from the tributaries of Lake Victoria in Tanzania and Uganda out to the Mediterranean Sea. Because of varying depths, boats can sail on only about 2,000 miles (3,217 km) of the river. The Nile flows through Rwanda, Uganda, Sudan, and Egypt. The river's water supply is crucial to the existence of these African countries. The Nile's precious water is used to irrigate crops and to generate electricity. The Aswan Dam and the Aswan High Dam—both located in Egypt—are used to store the autumn floodwater for later use. The Nile is also used to transport goods from city to city along the river.

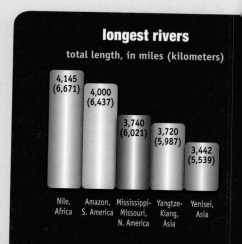

longest rivers

total length, in miles (kilometers)

4,145 (6,671)	4,000 (6,437)	3,740 (6,021)	3,720 (5,987)	3,442 (5,539)
Nile, Africa	Amazon, S. America	Mississippi-Missouri, N. America	Yangtze-Kiang, Asia	Yenisei, Asia

largest ocean
Pacific

The Pacific Ocean covers almost 64 million square miles (166 million sq km) and reaches 36,200 feet (11,000 m) below sea level at its greatest depth—the Mariana Trench (near the Philippines). In fact, this ocean is so large that it covers about one-third of the planet (more than all of Earth's land put together) and holds more than half of all the seawater on Earth. The United States could fit inside this ocean 18 times! Some of the major bodies of water included in the Pacific are the Bering Sea, the Coral Sea, the Philippine Sea, and the Gulf of Alaska.

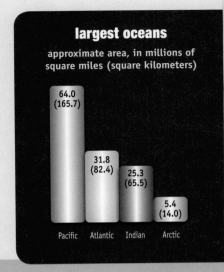

largest oceans

approximate area, in millions of square miles (square kilometers)

Pacific	Atlantic	Indian	Arctic
64.0 (165.7)	31.8 (82.4)	25.3 (65.5)	5.4 (14.0)

largest island

GREENLAND

Located in the North Atlantic Ocean, Greenland covers more than 840,000 square miles (2,175,600 sq km). Not including continents, it is the largest island in the world. Its jagged coastline is approximately 24,400 miles (39,267 km) long—about the same distance as Earth's circumference at the equator. Mountain chains are located on Greenland's east and west coasts, and the coastline is indented by fjords, or thin bodies of water bordered by steep cliffs. From north to south, the island stretches for about 1,660 miles (2,670 km). About 700,000 square miles (1,813,000 sq km) of this massive island are covered by a giant ice sheet. The island also contains the world's largest national park—Northeast Greenland National Park—with an area of 375,291 square miles (972,000 sq km).

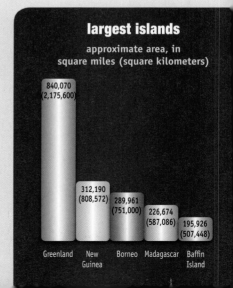

largest islands

approximate area, in
square miles (square kilometers)

Greenland	New Guinea	Borneo	Madagascar	Baffin Island
840,070 (2,175,600)	312,190 (808,572)	289,961 (751,000)	226,674 (587,086)	195,926 (507,448)

world's deepest sea trench
mariana trench

Located in the Pacific Ocean near Japan, the Mariana Trench is the deepest opening in Earth's crust at 35,787 feet (10,907 m). That's almost 7 miles (11.2 km). Mount Everest—the world's tallest mountain at 29,035 feet (8,850 m)—could easily fit inside. The deepest point on the trench is called the Challenger Deep, named after oceanographer Jacques Piccard's exploration vessel. It first mapped the trench in 1951. The trench is home to many types of crabs and fish, as well as more than 200 different types of microorganisms.

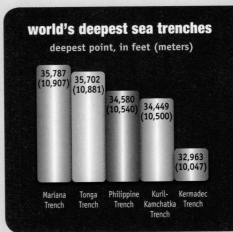

world's deepest sea trenches
deepest point, in feet (meters)

35,787 (10,907)	35,702 (10,881)	34,580 (10,540)	34,449 (10,500)	32,963 (10,047)
Mariana Trench	Tonga Trench	Philippine Trench	Kuril-Kamchatka Trench	Kermadec Trench

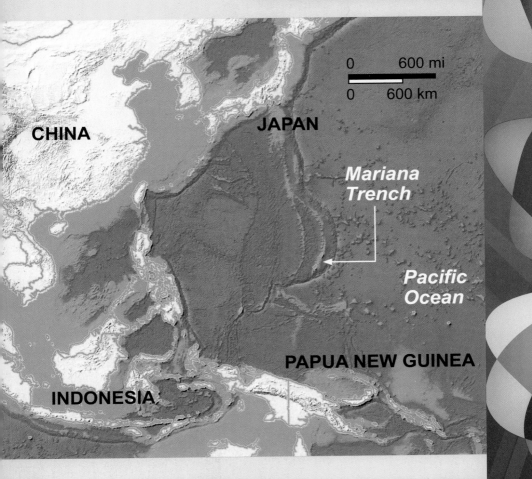

CHINA

JAPAN

0   600 mi
0   600 km

Mariana Trench

Pacific Ocean

PAPUA NEW GUINEA

INDONESIA

largest crustacean

GIANT SPIDER CRAB

The giant spider crab has a 12-foot (3.7 m) leg span. That's almost wide enough to take up two parking spaces! The crab's body measures about 15 inches (38.1 cm) wide. Its ten long legs are jointed, and the first pair has large claws at the end. The giant sea creature can weigh 35–44 pounds (16–20 kg). It feeds on dead animals and shellfish it finds on the ocean floor. Giant spider crabs live in the deep water of the Pacific Ocean off southern Japan.

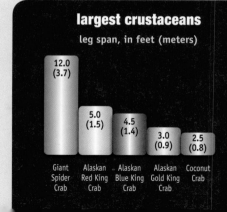

largest crustaceans

leg span, in feet (meters)

Giant Spider Crab	Alaskan Red King Crab	Alaskan Blue King Crab	Alaskan Gold King Crab	Coconut Crab
12.0 (3.7)	5.0 (1.5)	4.5 (1.4)	3.0 (0.9)	2.5 (0.8)

largest cephalopod

COLOSSAL SQUID

Living up to 6,000 feet (1,829 m) deep in the Antarctic Ocean, the colossal squid can grow to a length of 46 feet (14 m). That's about the same size as three SUVs! The squid, which is very rarely seen by people, can weigh about 1,500 pounds (681 kg). Its eyes are the size of dinner plates, and are the largest eyes in the animal kingdom. The colossal squid uses its 20-foot (6 m) long tentacles to catch its prey. In addition to the two tentacles, the giant cephalopod has eight arms. In the center of its body, the squid has a razor-sharp beak that it uses to shred its prey before eating it.

largest cephalopods
size, in feet (meters)

Colossal Squid	Giant Squid	Bigfin Squid	North Pacific Giant Octopus	Glass Squid
46 (14)	43 (13)	26 (8)	16 (5)	10 (3)

most dangerous shark

GreaT WHITe

With a total of 249 known unprovoked attacks on humans, great white sharks are the most dangerous predators in the sea. A great white can measure more than 20 feet (6.1 m) in length and weigh up to 3,800 pounds (1,723 kg). Because of the sharks' size, they can feed on large prey, including seals, dolphins, and even small whales. Often, when a human is attacked by a great white, it is because the shark has mistaken the person for its typical prey. The sharks make their homes in most waters throughout the world, but are most frequently found off the coasts of Australia, South Africa, California, and Mexico.

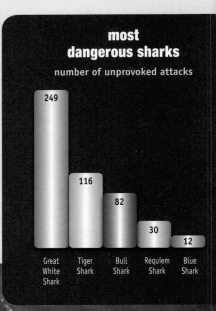

most dangerous sharks
number of unprovoked attacks

Great White Shark	Tiger Shark	Bull Shark	Requiem Shark	Blue Shark
249	116	82	30	12

biggest fish

WHALE SHARK

Although the average length of a whale shark is 30 feet (9 m), many have been known to reach up to 60 feet (18 m) long. That's the same length as two school buses! Whale sharks also weigh an average of 50,000 pounds (22,680 kg). As with most sharks, the females are larger than the males. Their mouths measure about 5 feet (1.5 m) long and contain about 3,000 teeth. Amazingly, these gigantic fish eat only microscopic plankton and tiny fish. They float near the surface looking for food.

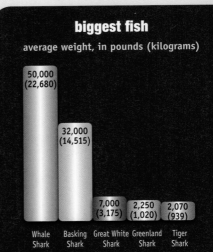

biggest fish

average weight, in pounds (kilograms)

Whale Shark	Basking Shark	Great White Shark	Greenland Shark	Tiger Shark
50,000 (22,680)	32,000 (14,515)	7,000 (3,175)	2,250 (1,020)	2,070 (939)

fastest fish

SAILFISH

A sailfish once grabbed a fishing line and dragged it 300 feet (91 m) away in just three seconds. That means it was swimming at an average speed of 69 miles (109 km) per hour—higher than the average speed limit on a highway! Sailfish are very large—they average 6 feet (1.8 m) long, but can grow up to 11 feet (3.4 m). Sailfish eat squid and surface-dwelling fish. Sometimes several sailfish will work together to catch their prey. They are found in both the Atlantic and Pacific oceans and prefer a water temperature of about 80°F (27°C).

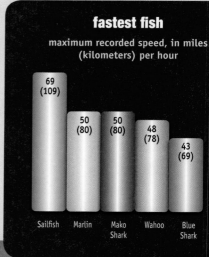

fastest fish

maximum recorded speed, in miles (kilometers) per hour

Sailfish	Marlin	Mako Shark	Wahoo	Blue Shark
69 (109)	50 (80)	50 (80)	48 (78)	43 (69)

biggest dolphin

orca

Although they are known as *killer whales*, the orca is actually a member of the dolphin family and can measure up to 32 feet (9.7 m) in length and weigh up to 6 tons (5.4 t). These powerful marine mammals are carnivores with 4-inch (1.6 cm) long teeth, and they feed mainly on seals, sea lions, and smaller whales. Orcas live in pods of up to 40 other whales, and pod members help one another round up prey. Killer whales can live for up to 80 years and are highly intelligent. Trainers in aquariums often work with orcas to perform live shows.

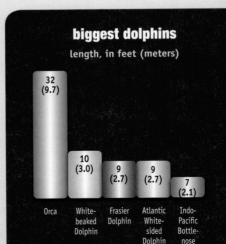

biggest dolphins

length, in feet (meters)

Orca	White-beaked Dolphin	Frasier Dolphin	Atlantic White-sided Dolphin	Indo-Pacific Bottle-nose Dolphin
32 (9.7)	10 (3.0)	9 (2.7)	9 (2.7)	7 (2.1)

heaviest marine mammal

BLUE WHALE

Blue whales are the largest animals that have ever inhabited Earth. They can weigh more than 143.3 tons (130 t) and measure over 100 feet (30 m) long. Amazingly, these gentle giants only eat krill—small shrimplike animals. A blue whale can eat about 4 tons (3.6 t) of krill each day in the summer, when food is plentiful. To catch the krill, a whale gulps as much as 17,000 gallons (64,600 L) of seawater into its mouth at one time. Then it uses its tongue—which can be as big as a car—to push the water back out. The krill get caught in hairs on the whale's baleen (a keratin structure that hangs down from the roof of the whale's mouth).

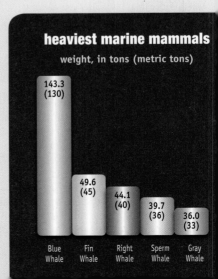

heaviest marine mammals
weight, in tons (metric tons)

Blue Whale	Fin Whale	Right Whale	Sperm Whale	Gray Whale
143.3 (130)	49.6 (45)	44.1 (40)	39.7 (36)	36.0 (33)

sperm whale

The sperm whale's brain is the largest marine mammal brain in the world, weighing more than 17 pounds (7.7 kg). That's more than five times the size of a human brain. Sperm whales can grow to about 60 feet (18 m) long and weigh up to 45 tons (41 t). The head makes up about one-third of the animal's body. Sperm whales can also dive deeper than any other whale, reaching depths of 3,300 feet (1,006 m) in search of squid. They can eat about 1 ton (0.9 t) of fish and squid daily. Sperm whales can be found in all oceans, and they generally live in pods of about a dozen adults and their offspring.

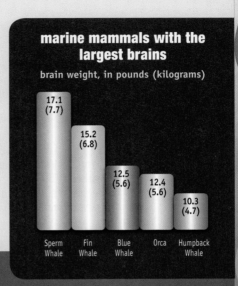

marine mammals with the largest brains

brain weight, in pounds (kilograms)

Sperm Whale	Fin Whale	Blue Whale	Orca	Humpback Whale
17.1 (7.7)	15.2 (6.8)	12.5 (5.6)	12.4 (5.6)	10.3 (4.7)

largest bird wingspan

marabou stork

With a wingspan that can reach up to 13 feet (4 m), the marabou stork has the largest wingspan of any bird. These large storks weigh up to 20 pounds (9 kg) and can grow up to 5 feet (150 cm) tall. Their long leg and toe bones are actually hollow. This adaptation is very important for flight because it makes the bird lighter. Although marabous eat insects, small mammals, and fish, the majority of their food is carrion—meat that is already dead. In fact, the stork's head and neck do not have any feathers. This helps the bird stay clean as it sticks its head into carcasses to pick out scraps of food.

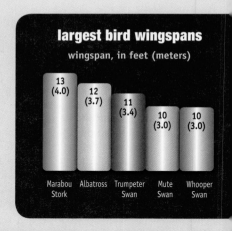

largest bird wingspans

wingspan, in feet (meters)

Marabou Stork	Albatross	Trumpeter Swan	Mute Swan	Whooper Swan
13 (4.0)	12 (3.7)	11 (3.4)	10 (3.0)	10 (3.0)

biggest penguin

emperor penguin

Emperor penguins are giants among their species, growing to a height of 44 inches (111.7 cm) and weighing up to 80 pounds (37 kg). These penguins are the only animals that spend the entire winter on the open ice in Antarctica, withstanding temperatures as low as -75°F (-60°C). The female penguin lays a 1-pound (0.5 kg) egg on the ice, and then goes off to hunt for weeks at a time. The male penguin scoops up the egg, and keeps it warm on his feet below his toasty belly. When the eggs hatch, the females return with food.

biggest penguins

height in inches (centimeters)

Emperor Penguin	King Penguin	Gentoo Penguin	Yellow-eyed Penguin	Chinstrap Penguin
44 (111.7)	37 (93.9)	35 (88.9)	31 (78.7)	30 (76.2)

arctic tern

The arctic tern migrates from Maine to the coast of Africa, and then on to Antarctica, flying some 22,000 miles (35,406 km) a year. That's almost the same distance as the Earth's circumference. Some don't complete the journey, however—young terns fly the first half of the journey with their parents, but remain in the Antarctic for a year or two. When they have matured, the birds fly back to Maine and the surrounding areas. Scientists are puzzled about how these birds remember the way back after only making the journey once, so early in their lives.

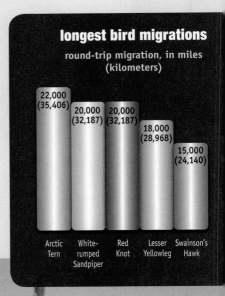

longest bird migrations
round-trip migration, in miles (kilometers)

Arctic Tern	White-rumped Sandpiper	Red Knot	Lesser Yellowleg	Swainson's Hawk
22,000 (35,406)	20,000 (32,187)	20,000 (32,187)	18,000 (28,968)	15,000 (24,140)

A pair of juvenile bald eagles near their nest

bird that builds the largest nest

BaLD eaGLe

With a nest that can measure 8 feet (2.4 m) wide and 16 feet (4.9 m) deep, bald eagles have plenty of room to move around. These birds of prey have wingspans of up to 7.5 feet (2.3 m) and need a home that they can nest in comfortably. By carefully constructing their nest with sticks, branches, and plant material, a pair of bald eagles can balance their home—which can weigh up to 4,000 pounds (1,814 kg)—on the top of a tree or cliff. These nests are usually located by rivers or coastlines, the birds' watery hunting grounds. Called an aerie, this home will be used for the rest of the eagles' lives.

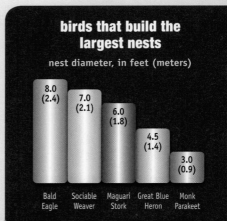

birds that build the largest nests

nest diameter, in feet (meters)

Bald Eagle	Sociable Weaver	Maguari Stork	Great Blue Heron	Monk Parakeet
8.0 (2.4)	7.0 (2.1)	6.0 (1.8)	4.5 (1.4)	3.0 (0.9)

animals

largest bird egg

OSTRICH EGG

Ostriches—the world's largest birds—can lay eggs that measure 5 inches by 6 inches (13 cm by 16 cm) and weigh up to 4 pounds (1.8 kg). In fact, just one ostrich egg weighs as much as 24 chicken eggs! The egg yolk makes up one-third of the volume. Although the eggshell is only 0.08 inches (2 mm) thick, it is tough enough to withstand the weight of a 345-pound (157 kg) ostrich. An ostrich hen can lay from 10 to 70 eggs each year. Females are usually able to recognize their own eggs, even when they are mixed in with those of other females in their shared nest.

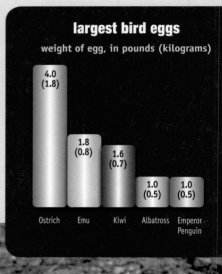

largest bird eggs

weight of egg, in pounds (kilograms)

Ostrich	Emu	Kiwi	Albatross	Emperor Penguin
4.0 (1.8)	1.8 (0.8)	1.6 (0.7)	1.0 (0.5)	1.0 (0.5)

Sockeye salmon

most endangered US animal group

FISHES

There are 78 species of fish that are currently endangered in the United States. A species is considered endangered if it is in danger of becoming extinct. In addition, there are another 71 fish species that are considered threatened. Out of the 149 endangered and threatened fish species, there is a recovery plan in place for 101 of them. The main reasons for the decline in some species' populations are overfishing, water pollution, and loss of habitat. Some of the most well-known endangered fish include the Atlantic salmon, the steelhead trout, the sockeye salmon, and the Atlantic sturgeon.

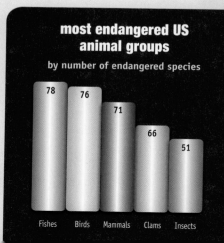

most endangered US animal groups

by number of endangered species

Fishes	Birds	Mammals	Clams	Insects
78	76	71	66	51

biggest bear

Polar Bear

A massive male polar bear can weigh in at up to 1,600 pounds (726 kg), which is about the same weight as ten grown men. Females are smaller than the males, and the weight of both genders fluctuates when food is scarce. The 8-foot (2.4 m) tall animals live in the frigid Arctic, patrolling the ice and surrounding water for food. Polar bears are excellent swimmers, and can travel more than 100 miles (161 km) in icy water searching for seals to eat. Their dense coats protect them from snow, ice, and wind. They even have thick strips of fur on their paws to insulate their feet and help them grip the ice.

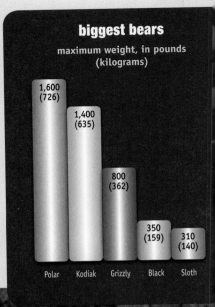

biggest bears
maximum weight, in pounds (kilograms)

Polar	Kodiak	Grizzly	Black	Sloth
1,600 (726)	1,400 (635)	800 (362)	350 (159)	310 (140)

heaviest land mammal

african elephant

Weighing in at up to 14,430 pounds (6,545 kg) and measuring approximately 24 feet (7.3 m) long, African elephants are truly humongous. Even at their great size, they are strictly vegetarian. They will, however, eat up to 500 pounds (226 kg) of vegetation a day! Their two tusks—which are actually elongated teeth—grow continuously during their lives and can reach about 9 feet (2.7 m) in length. Elephants live in small groups of 8 to 15 family members with one female (called a cow) as the leader.

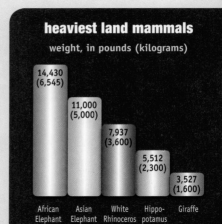

heaviest land mammals

weight, in pounds (kilograms)

African Elephant	Asian Elephant	White Rhinoceros	Hippo-potamus	Giraffe
14,430 (6,545)	11,000 (5,000)	7,937 (3,600)	5,512 (2,300)	3,527 (1,600)

largest rodent

capybara

Capybaras reach an average length of 4 feet (1.2 m), stand about 20 inches (51 cm) tall, and weigh 75–150 pounds (34–68 kg)! That's about the same size as a Labrador retriever. Also known as water hogs and carpinchos, capybaras are found in South and Central America, where they spend much of their time in groups, looking for food. They are strictly vegetarian and have been known to raid gardens for melons and squash. Their partially webbed feet make capybaras excellent swimmers. They can dive down to the bottom of a lake or river to find plants and stay there for up to five minutes.

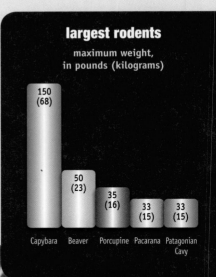

largest rodents

maximum weight,
in pounds (kilograms)

Capybara	Beaver	Porcupine	Pacarana	Patagonian Cavy
150 (68)	50 (23)	35 (16)	33 (15)	33 (15)

biggest wolf

arctic WOLF

The gray wolf is the largest member of the Canidae family, which also includes foxes, coyotes, jackals, and dogs. There are five subspecies of the gray wolf, and of them, the Arctic wolf is the largest. Measuring 32 inches (81 cm) long and weighing up to 175 pounds (79 kg), these meat-eating mammals live and hunt in packs. Working together, they can take down prey much larger than themselves, including deer, moose, and caribou. Gray wolves can chase prey for more than 20 minutes, sometimes reaching speeds of 35 miles (56 km) per hour. They live throughout North America and in parts of Europe and Asia.

biggest wolves

maximum weight,
in pounds (kilograms)

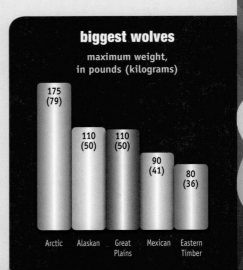

Arctic	Alaskan	Great Plains	Mexican	Eastern Timber
175 (79)	110 (50)	110 (50)	90 (41)	80 (36)

fastest land mammal

CHEETAH

For short spurts, these sleek mammals can reach a speed of 65 miles (105 km) per hour. They can accelerate from 0 to 40 miles (64 km) per hour in just three strides. Their quickness easily enables these large African cats to outrun their prey. All other African cats can only stalk their prey because they lack the cheetah's amazing speed. Unlike the paws of all other cats, cheetah paws do not have skin sheaths (thin protective coverings). Their claws, therefore, cannot be retracted.

fastest land mammals

speed, in miles (kilometers) per hour

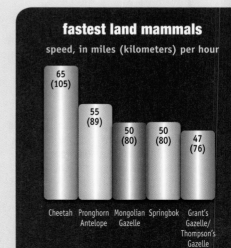

65 (105)	55 (89)	50 (80)	50 (80)	47 (76)
Cheetah	Pronghorn Antelope	Mongolian Gazelle	Springbok	Grant's Gazelle/ Thompson's Gazelle

TIGER

Although tigers average about 448 pounds (203 kg), some of these big cats can grow to 725 pounds (328 kg) and measure 6 feet (1.8 m) long—not including a 3-foot (0.9 m) tail. Tigers that live in colder habitats are usually larger than ones that live in warmer areas. These giant cats hunt at night, and can easily bring down a full-grown antelope alone. One tiger can eat about 60 pounds (27 kg) of meat in just one night. The five types of tigers are Bengal, Indochinese, South China, Sumatran, and Siberian. All tiger species are endangered, mostly because of over-hunting and loss of habitat due to farming and logging.

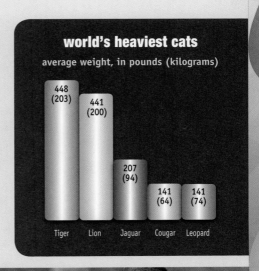

world's heaviest cats

average weight, in pounds (kilograms)

Tiger	Lion	Jaguar	Cougar	Leopard
448 (203)	441 (200)	207 (94)	141 (64)	141 (74)

largest bat

GIANT FLYING FOX

The giant flying fox—a member of the megabat family—can have a wingspan of up to 6 feet (1.8 m). These furry mammals average just 7 wing beats per second, but can travel more than 40 miles (64 km) a night in search of food. Unlike smaller bats, which use echolocation, flying foxes rely on their acute vision and sense of smell to locate fruit, pollen, and nectar. Flying foxes got their name because their faces resemble a fox's face. Megabats live in the tropical areas of Africa, Asia, and Australia.

largest bats

wingspan, in feet (meters)

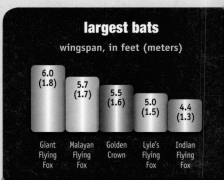

Giant Flying Fox	Malayan Flying Fox	Golden Crown	Lyle's Flying Fox	Indian Flying Fox
6.0 (1.8)	5.7 (1.7)	5.5 (1.6)	5.0 (1.5)	4.4 (1.3)

tallest land animal

Giraffe

Giraffes are the giants among mammals, growing up to 18 feet (5.5 m) in height. That means an average giraffe could look through the window of a two-story building! A giraffe's neck is 18 times longer than a human's, but both mammals have exactly the same number of neck bones. A giraffe's long legs enable it to outrun most of its enemies. When cornered, a giraffe's long legs have the strength to kill a lion with a single kick to the head.

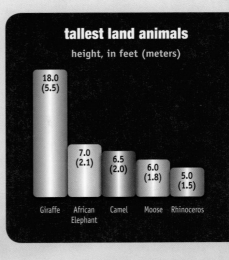

tallest land animals
height, in feet (meters)

Giraffe	African Elephant	Camel	Moose	Rhinoceros
18.0 (5.5)	7.0 (2.1)	6.5 (2.0)	6.0 (1.8)	5.0 (1.5)

world's heaviest marsupial

red kangaroo

Full-grown male red kangaroos can grow up to 6 feet (1.8 m) tall and weigh around 200 pounds (90.7 kg), while females are slightly smaller. Females can travel up to 30 miles (48 km) per hour and leap up to 10 feet (3 m) high. At top speed, a single bound can cover 39 feet (12 m). Kangaroos are very social and live in herds called mobs. They are herbivores and feed on many different types of plants. Red kangaroos are commonly found in open woodland or savannahs of inland Australia. They can survive on very little water.

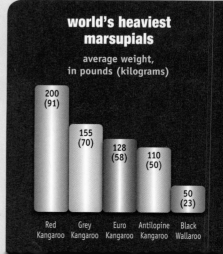

world's heaviest marsupials

average weight, in pounds (kilograms)

Red Kangaroo	Grey Kangaroo	Euro Kangaroo	Antilopine Kangaroo	Black Wallaroo
200 (91)	155 (70)	128 (58)	110 (50)	50 (23)

largest primate

Gorilla

Gorillas are the kings of the primate family, weighing in at up to 400 pounds (181 kg). The eastern lowland gorilla is the largest of the four subspecies of gorillas, which also include western lowland, Cross River, and mountain. All gorillas are found in Africa, and all but mountain gorillas live in tropical forests. They are mostly plant eaters, but will occasionally eat small animals. An adult male gorilla can eat up to 45 pounds (32 kg) of food in a day. Gorillas live in groups of about 4 to 12 family members, and can live for about 35 years in the wild.

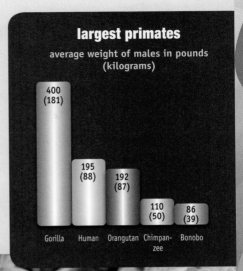

largest primates
average weight of males in pounds (kilograms)

Gorilla	Human	Orangutan	Chimpan-zee	Bonobo
400 (181)	195 (88)	192 (87)	110 (50)	86 (39)

deadliest amphibian

POISON
Dart Frog

Poison dart frogs are found mostly in the tropical rain forests of Central and South America, where they live on the moist land. These lethal amphibians have enough poison to kill up to 20 humans. A dart frog's poison is so effective that native Central and South Americans sometimes coat their hunting arrows or hunting darts with it. These brightly colored frogs can be yellow, orange, red, green, blue, or any combination of these colors. They measure only 0.5–2 inches (1–5 cm) long. There are approximately 75 different species of poison dart frogs.

some of the deadliest amphibians
risk of fatality

Extreme	High	Medium	Medium	Medium
Poison Dart Frog	Black and Yellow Spotted Frog	Fire-bellied Toad	European Salamander	Cane Toad

longest snake

reticulated PYTHON

Some adult reticulated pythons can grow to 27 feet (8.2 m) long, but most reach an average length of 17 feet (5 m). That's almost the length of an average school bus! These pythons live mostly in Asia, from Myanmar to Indonesia to the Philippines. The python has teeth that curve backward to hold its prey still. It hunts mainly at night and will eat mammals and birds. Reticulated pythons are slow-moving creatures that kill their prey by constriction, or strangulation.

longest snakes

maximum length, in feet (meters)

Reticulated Python	Anaconda	Rock Python	King Cobra	Oriental Rat Snake
27.0 (8.2)	25.0 (7.6)	24.6 (7.5)	17.7 (5.4)	12.2 (3.7)

snake with the longest fangs

GaBOON VIPer

The fangs of a Gaboon viper measure 2 inches (5.1 cm) in length! These giant fangs fold up against the snake's mouth so it does not pierce its own skin. When it is ready to strike its prey, the fangs snap down into position. The snake can grow up to 7 feet (2 m) long and weigh 18 pounds (8 kg). It is found in Africa and is perfectly camouflaged for hunting on the ground beneath leaves and grasses. The Gaboon viper's poison is not as toxic as some other snakes', but it is quite dangerous because of the amount of poison it can inject at one time. The snake is not very aggressive, however, and usually attacks only when bothered.

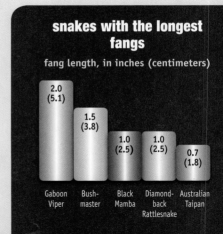

snakes with the longest fangs

fang length, in inches (centimeters)

2.0 (5.1)	1.5 (3.8)	1.0 (2.5)	1.0 (2.5)	0.7 (1.8)
Gaboon Viper	Bush-master	Black Mamba	Diamond-back Rattlesnake	Australian Taipan

Black Mamba

With just one bite, an African black mamba snake releases a venom powerful enough to kill up to 200 humans. A bite from this snake is almost always fatal if it is not treated immediately. This large member of the cobra family grows to about 14 feet (4.3 m) long. In addition to its deadly poison, it is a very aggressive snake. It will raise its body off the ground when it feels threatened. It then spreads its hood and strikes swiftly at its prey with its long front teeth. A black mamba is also very fast—it can move along at about 7 miles (11.7 km) per hour for short bursts.

deadliest snakes

human deaths possible per bite

Black Mamba	Taipan	Russell's Viper	Common Krait	Forest Cobra
200	170	150	60	50

largest amphibian

CHINESE GIANT SALAMANDER

With a length of 6 feet (1.8 m) and a weight of 55 pounds (25 kg), Chinese giant salamanders rule the amphibian world. This salamander has a large head, but its eyes and nostrils are small. It has short legs, a long tail, and very smooth skin. This large creature can be found in the streams of northeastern, central, and southern China. It feeds on fish, frogs, crabs, and snakes. The Chinese giant salamander will not hunt its prey. It waits until a potential meal wanders too close and then grabs it in its mouth. Because many people enjoy the taste of the salamander's meat, it is often hunted and its population is shrinking.

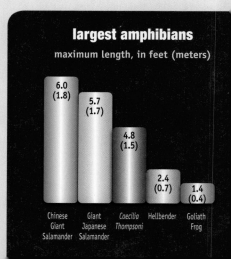

largest amphibians

maximum length, in feet (meters)

Chinese Giant Salamander	Giant Japanese Salamander	Caecilia Thompsoni	Hellbender	Goliath Frog
6.0 (1.8)	5.7 (1.7)	4.8 (1.5)	2.4 (0.7)	1.4 (0.4)

GOLIATH FROG

The Goliath frog has a body that measures 13 inches (33 cm) long, but when its legs are extended, its total body length can increase to more than 2.5 feet (0.76 m). These gigantic frogs can weigh around 7 pounds (3 kg). Oddly enough, the eggs and tadpoles of this species are the same size as smaller frogs'. Goliath frogs are found only in the western African countries of Equatorial Guinea and Cameroon. They live in rivers that are surrounded by dense rain forests. These huge amphibians are becoming endangered, mostly because their rain forest homes are being destroyed.

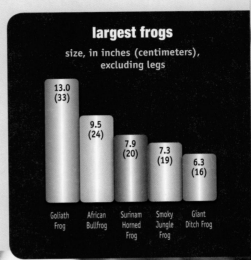

largest frogs

size, in inches (centimeters), excluding legs

Goliath Frog	African Bullfrog	Surinam Horned Frog	Smoky Jungle Frog	Giant Ditch Frog
13.0 (33)	9.5 (24)	7.9 (20)	7.3 (19)	6.3 (16)

largest lizard

KOMODO DRAGON

With a length of 10 feet (3 m) and a weight of 300 pounds (136 kg), Komodo dragons are the largest lizards roaming the earth. A Komodo dragon has a long neck and tail, and strong legs. These members of the monitor family are found mainly on Komodo Island, located in the Lesser Sunda Islands of Indonesia. Komodos are dangerous and have even been known to attack and kill humans. A Komodo uses its sense of smell to locate food, using its long, yellow tongue. A Komodo can consume 80 percent of its body weight in just one meal!

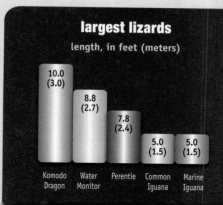

largest lizards

length, in feet (meters)

Komodo Dragon	Water Monitor	Perentie	Common Iguana	Marine Iguana
10.0 (3.0)	8.8 (2.7)	7.8 (2.4)	5.0 (1.5)	5.0 (1.5)

largest reptile
saltwater crocodile

Saltwater crocodiles can grow to 22 feet (6.7 m) long. That's about twice the length of the average car! However, males usually measure only about 17 feet (5 m) long, and females normally reach about 10 feet (3 m) in length. A large adult will feed on buffalo, monkeys, cattle, wild boar, and other large mammals. Saltwater crocodiles are found throughout the East Indies and Australia. Despite their name, saltwater crocodiles can also be found in freshwater and swamps. Some other common names for this species are the estuarine crocodile and the Indo-Pacific crocodile.

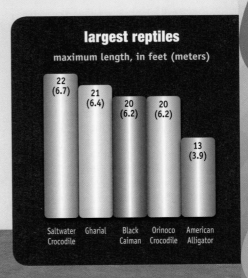

largest reptiles

maximum length, in feet (meters)

Saltwater Crocodile	Gharial	Black Caiman	Orinoco Crocodile	American Alligator
22 (6.7)	21 (6.4)	20 (6.2)	20 (6.2)	13 (3.9)

largest spider

GOLIATH BIRDEATER

A Goliath birdeater is about the same size as a dinner plate—it can grow to a total length of 11 inches (28 cm) and weigh about 6 ounces (170 g). A Goliath's spiderlings are also big—they can have a 6-inch (15 cm) leg span just one year after hatching. These giant tarantulas are found mostly in the rain forests of Guyana, Suriname, Brazil, and Venezuela. The Goliath birdeater's name is misleading—they commonly eat insects and small reptiles. Similar to other tarantula species, the Goliath birdeater lives in a burrow. The spider will wait by the opening to ambush prey that gets too close.

largest spiders

length, in inches (centimeters)

Goliath Birdeater	Salmon Pink Birdeater	Slate Red Ornamental	King Baboon	Colombian Giant Redleg
11.0 (28)	10.5 (27)	9.0 (23)	8.0 (20)	8.0 (20)

fastest-flying insect

HAWK MOTH

The average hawk moth—which got its name from its swift and steady flight—can cruise along at speeds over 33 miles (53 km) per hour. That's faster than the average speed limit on most city streets! Although they are found throughout the world, most live in tropical climates. Also known as the sphinx moth and the hummingbird moth, this large insect can have a wingspan that reaches up to 8 inches (20 cm). The insect also has a good memory and may return to the same flowers at the same time each day.

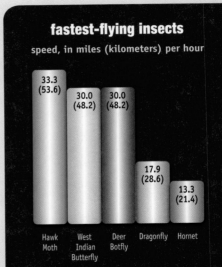

fastest-flying insects

speed, in miles (kilometers) per hour

Hawk Moth	West Indian Butterfly	Deer Botfly	Dragonfly	Hornet
33.3 (53.6)	30.0 (48.2)	30.0 (48.2)	17.9 (28.6)	13.3 (21.4)

fastest-running insect

australian tiger beetle

Australian tiger beetles can zip along at about 5.7 miles (9.2 km) per hour—that's about 170 body lengths per second! If a human could run at the same pace, he or she would run about 340 miles (547.2 km) per hour. Australian tiger beetles use their terrific speed to run down prey. Once a meal has been caught, the beetle chews it up in its powerful jaws and coats it in digestive juice. When the prey has become soft, the tiger beetle rolls it together and eats it. These fierce beetles, which got their name from their skillful hunting, will also bite humans when provoked.

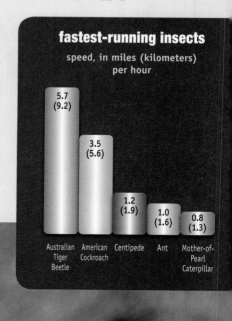

fastest-running insects

speed, in miles (kilometers) per hour

Australian Tiger Beetle	American Cockroach	Centipede	Ant	Mother-of-Pearl Caterpillar
5.7 (9.2)	3.5 (5.6)	1.2 (1.9)	1.0 (1.6)	0.8 (1.3)

longest insect migration
MONARCH BUTTERFLY

Millions of monarch butterflies travel to Mexico from all parts of North America every fall, flying as far as 2,700 miles (4,345 km). Once there, they will huddle together in the trees and wait out the cold weather. In spring and summer, most butterflies only live four or five weeks as adults, but in the fall, a special generation of monarchs is born. These butterflies will live for about seven months and participate in the great migration to Mexico. Scientists are studying these butterflies in the hope of learning how the insects know where and when to migrate to a place they have never visited before.

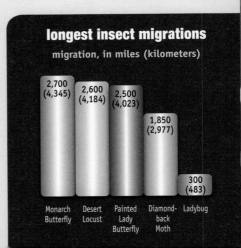

longest insect migrations

migration, in miles (kilometers)

Monarch Butterfly	Desert Locust	Painted Lady Butterfly	Diamond-back Moth	Ladybug
2,700 (4,345)	2,600 (4,184)	2,500 (4,023)	1,850 (2,977)	300 (483)

DOG

There are 46.3 million households across the United States that own one or more dogs. That means that about 39 percent of homes in America have a pooch residing there. About 28 percent of these families own two dogs, while another 12 percent own three or more. When it comes to finding a dog, approximately 21 percent of families head to a shelter to adopt one. Those who prefer purebreds tend to choose Labrador retrievers, German shepherds, and Yorkshire terriers. Some of the most popular dog names include Max, Buddy, Rocky, and Bailey.

most common pets in the united states

number of US households that own pets, in millions

Dog	Cat	Freshwater Fish	Bird	Other Small Animal
46.3	38.9	11.9	5.7	5.0

most popular dog breed in the united states
LaBRaDOR ReTRIeVeR

Labrador retrievers are top dog in the United States! In 2011, the American Kennel Club recorded more purebred dog registrations for labs than any other dog in the United States. Labs are very popular with families because of their gentle nature, and they are popular with hunters because of their retrieving skills. A very intelligent breed, Labrador retrievers can be trained to work in law enforcement or as guide dogs. They come in three colors—yellow, black, and brown—and are medium-size athletic dogs. They are considered by the American Kennel Club to be part of the sporting class.

most popular dog breeds in the united states
american kennel club rank

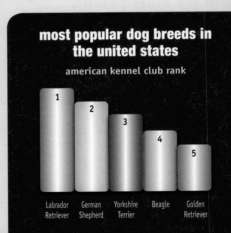

Labrador Retriever	German Shepherd	Yorkshire Terrier	Beagle	Golden Retriever
1	2	3	4	5

most popular cat breed in the united states

persian

The Cat Fanciers' Association—the world's largest registry of pedigree cats—ranks the Persian as the most popular cat in the country. These flat-faced cats are known for their gentle personalities, which make them popular family pets. Persians come in many colors, including silver, golden, smoke, and tabby. They have long hair, which requires continuous grooming and maintenance. These pets, like most other cat breeds, can live as long as 15 years.

most popular cat breeds in the united states
cat fanciers' association rank

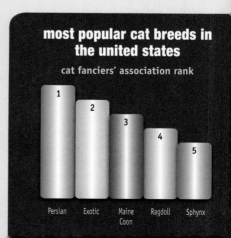

Persian	Exotic	Maine Coon	Ragdoll	Sphynx
1	2	3	4	5

MOUNT rainier

Mount Rainier had a record snowfall of 1,224 inches (3,109 cm) between February 1971 and February 1972. That's enough snow to cover a ten-story building! Located in the Cascade Mountains of Washington State, Mount Rainier is actually a volcano buried under 35 square miles (90.7 sq km) of snow and ice. The mountain, which covers about 100 square miles (259 sq km), reaches a height of 14,410 feet (4,392 m). Its three peaks include Liberty Cap, Point Success, and Columbia Crest. Mount Rainier National Park was established in 1899.

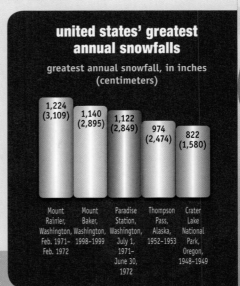

united states' greatest annual snowfalls

greatest annual snowfall, in inches (centimeters)

Snowfall	Location
1,224 (3,109)	Mount Rainier, Washington, Feb. 1971–Feb. 1972
1,140 (2,895)	Mount Baker, Washington, 1998–1999
1,122 (2,849)	Paradise Station, Washington, July 1, 1971–June 30, 1972
974 (2,474)	Thompson Pass, Alaska, 1952–1953
822 (1,580)	Crater Lake National Park, Oregon, 1948–1949

coldest inhabited place

resolute

The residents of Resolute, Canada, have to bundle up—the average temperature is just -11.6°F (-24.2°C). Located on the northeast shore of Resolute Bay on the south coast of Cornwallis Island, the community is commonly the starting point for expeditions to the North Pole. In the winter it can stay dark for 24 hours, and in the summer it can stay light during the entire night. Only about 200 people brave the climate year-round, but the area is becoming quite popular with tourists.

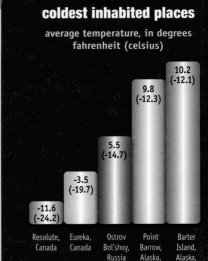

coldest inhabited places
average temperature, in degrees fahrenheit (celsius)

Resolute, Canada	Eureka, Canada	Ostrov Bol'shoy, Russia	Point Barrow, Alaska, USA	Barter Island, Alaska, USA
-11.6 (-24.2)	-3.5 (-19.7)	5.5 (-14.7)	9.8 (-12.3)	10.2 (-12.1)

DALLOL

Throughout the year, temperatures in Dallol, Ethiopia, average 93.2°F (34°C). Dallol is at the northernmost tip of the Great Rift Valley. The Dallol Depression reaches 328 feet (100 m) below sea level, making it the lowest point below sea level that is not covered by water. The area also has several active volcanoes. The only people to inhabit the region are the Afar, who have adapted to the harsh conditions there. For instance, to collect water, the women build covered stone piles and wait for condensation to form on the rocks.

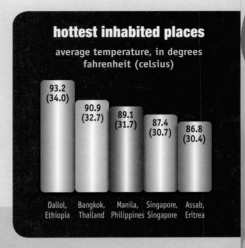

hottest inhabited places

average temperature, in degrees fahrenheit (celsius)

Dallol, Ethiopia	Bangkok, Thailand	Manila, Philippines	Singapore, Singapore	Assab, Eritrea
93.2 (34.0)	90.9 (32.7)	89.1 (31.7)	87.4 (30.7)	86.8 (30.4)

wettest inhabited place

Lloro

Umbrellas are in constant use in Lloro, Colombia, where the average annual rainfall totals about 524 inches (1,328 cm). That's about 1.4 inches (3.5 cm) a day, totaling more than 43 feet (13 m) a year! Located in the northwestern part of the country, Lloro is near the Pacific Ocean and the Caribbean Sea. Trade winds help bring lots of moisture from the coasts to this tropical little town, creating the humidity and precipitation that soak this lowland. Lloro is home to about 7,000 people.

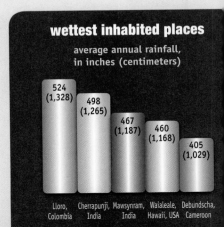

wettest inhabited places

average annual rainfall, in inches (centimeters)

524 (1,328) — Lloro, Colombia
498 (1,265) — Cherrapunji, India
467 (1,187) — Mawsynram, India
460 (1,168) — Waialeale, Hawaii, USA
405 (1,029) — Debundscha, Cameroon

driest inhabited place

aswan

Each year, only 0.02 inches (0.5 mm) of rain falls on Aswan, Egypt. In the country's sunniest and southernmost city, summer temperatures can reach a blistering 114°F (46°C). Aswan is located on the west bank of the Nile River, and it has a very busy marketplace that is also popular with tourists. The Aswan High Dam, at 12,565 feet (3,830 m) long, is the city's most famous landmark. It produces the majority of Egypt's power in the form of hydroelectricity.

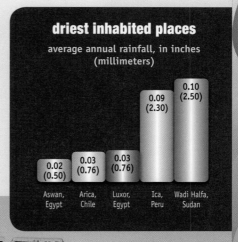

driest inhabited places

average annual rainfall, in inches (millimeters)

Aswan, Egypt	Arica, Chile	Luxor, Egypt	Ica, Peru	Wadi Halfa, Sudan
0.02 (0.50)	0.03 (0.76)	0.03 (0.76)	0.09 (2.30)	0.10 (2.50)

place with the fastest winds

Barrow Island

On April 12, 1996, Cyclone Olivia blew through Barrow Island in Australia and created a wind gust that reached 253 miles (407 km) an hour. Barrow Island is about 30 miles (48 km) off the coast of Western Australia and is home to many endangered species, such as dugongs and green turtles. The dry, sandy land measures about 78 square miles (202 sq km) and is the second-largest island in Western Australia. Barrow Island also has hundreds of oil wells and is a top source of oil for the country. The island has produced more than 300 million barrels of oil since 1967.

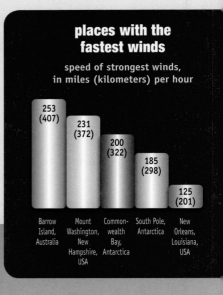

places with the fastest winds

speed of strongest winds, in miles (kilometers) per hour

Barrow Island, Australia	Mount Washington, New Hampshire, USA	Common-wealth Bay, Antarctica	South Pole, Antarctica	New Orleans, Louisiana, USA
253 (407)	231 (372)	200 (322)	185 (298)	125 (201)

tallest cactus

saguaro

Many saguaro cacti grow to a height of 50 feet (15 m), but some have actually reached 75 feet (23 m). That's taller than a seven-story building! Saguaros start out quite small and grow very slowly. A saguaro reaches only about 1 inch (2.5 cm) high during its first 10 years. It will not bloom until it is between 50 and 75 years old. By this time, the cactus has a strong root system that can support about 9–10 tons (8–9 t) of growth. Its spines can measure up to 2.5 inches (5 cm) long. Saguaro cacti live for about 170 years. The giant cacti can be found from southeastern California to southern Arizona.

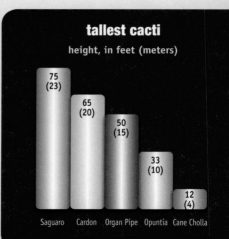

tallest cacti
height, in feet (meters)

Saguaro	Cardon	Organ Pipe	Opuntia	Cane Cholla
75 (23)	65 (20)	50 (15)	33 (10)	12 (4)

tallest tree

CALIFORNIA REDWOOD

Growing in both California and southern Oregon, California redwoods can reach a height of 385 feet (117 m). Their trunks can grow up to 25 feet (8 m) in diameter. The tallest redwood on record is more than 60 feet (18 m) taller than the Statue of Liberty. Amazingly, this giant tree grows from a seed the size of a tomato. Some redwoods are believed to be more than 2,000 years old. The trees' thick bark and foliage protect them from natural hazards such as insects and fires.

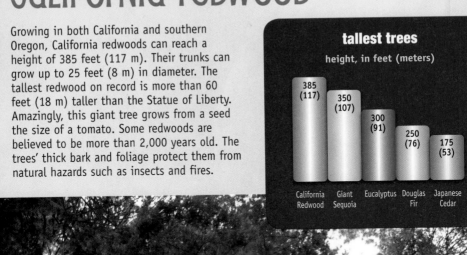

tallest trees

height, in feet (meters)

385 (117)	California Redwood
350 (107)	Giant Sequoia
300 (91)	Eucalyptus
250 (76)	Douglas Fir
175 (53)	Japanese Cedar

most poisonous mushroom

DEATH CAP

Death cap mushrooms are members of the Amanita family, which are among the most dangerous mushrooms in the world. The death cap contains deadly peptide toxins that cause rapid loss of bodily fluids and intense thirst. Within six hours, the poison shuts down the kidneys, liver, and central nervous system, causing coma and—in more than 50 percent of cases—death. Estimates of the number of poisonous mushroom species range from 80 to 2,000. Most experts agree, however, that at least 100 varieties will cause severe symptoms and even death if eaten.

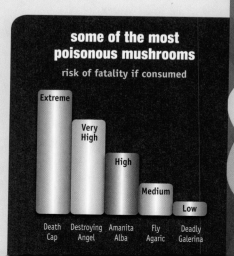

some of the most poisonous mushrooms

risk of fatality if consumed

Death Cap	Destroying Angel	Amanita Alba	Fly Agaric	Deadly Galerina
Extreme	Very High	High	Medium	Low

largest flower

rafflesia

The blossoms of the giant rafflesia—or stinking corpse lily—can reach 36 inches (91 cm) in diameter and weigh up to 25 pounds (11 kg). Its petals can grow 1.5 feet (0.5 m) long and 1 inch (2.5 cm) thick. There are 16 different species of rafflesia. This endangered plant is found only in the rain forests of Borneo and Sumatra. It lives inside the bark of host vines and is noticeable only when its flowers break through to blossom. The large, reddish purple flowers give off a smell similar to rotting meat, which attracts insects that help spread the rafflesia's pollen.

largest flowers
size, in inches (centimeters)

Rafflesia	Sunflower	Giant Water Lily	Brazilian Dutchman	Magnolia
36 (91)	19 (48)	18 (46)	14 (36)	10 (25)

highest tsunami wave since 1900

LITUYA BAY

A 1,720-foot (524 m) tsunami wave crashed down in Lituya Bay, Alaska, on July 9, 1958. Located in Glacier Bay National Park, the tsunami was caused by a massive landslide that was triggered by an 8.3-magnitude earthquake. The water from the bay covered 5 square miles (13 sq km) of land and traveled inland as far as 3,600 feet (1,097 m). Millions of trees were washed away. Amazingly, because the area was very isolated and the coastline was sheltered by coves, only two people died when their fishing boat sank.

highest tsunami waves since 1900

height of wave, in feet (meters)

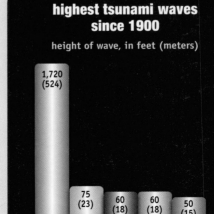

Lituya Bay, Alaska, USA, 1958	Chile, 1960	Japan, 2011	Philippines, 1960	Southern Asia, 2004
1,720 (524)	75 (23)	60 (18)	60 (18)	50 (15)

CHILE

An explosive earthquake measuring 9.5 on the Richter scale rocked the coast of Chile on May 22, 1960. This is equal to the intensity of about 60,000 hydrogen bombs. Some 2,000 people were killed and another 3,000 injured. The death toll was fairly low because the foreshocks frightened people into the streets. When the massive jolt came, many of the buildings that collapsed were already empty. The coastal towns of Valdivia and Puerto Montt suffered the most damage because they were closest to the epicenter— located about 100 miles (161 km) offshore. On February 27, 2010, Chile was rocked by another huge earthquake (8.8 magnitude), but the loss of life and property was much less than from previous quakes.

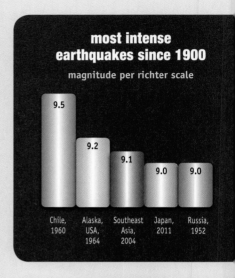

most intense earthquakes since 1900

magnitude per richter scale

Chile, 1960	Alaska, USA, 1964	Southeast Asia, 2004	Japan, 2011	Russia, 1952
9.5	9.2	9.1	9.0	9.0

most destructive flood since 1900

Hurricane Katrina

The pounding rain and storm surges of Hurricane Katrina resulted in catastrophic flooding that cost about $60 billion. The storm formed in late August 2005 over the Bahamas, moved across Florida, and finally hit Louisiana on August 29 as a category-3 storm. The storm surge from the Gulf of Mexico flooded the state, as well as neighboring Alabama and Mississippi. Many levees could not hold back the massive amounts of water, and entire towns were destroyed. In total, some 1,800 people lost their lives.

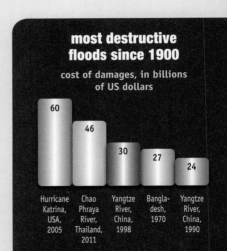

most destructive floods since 1900

cost of damages, in billions of US dollars

60	46	30	27	24
Hurricane Katrina, USA, 2005	Chao Phraya River, Thailand, 2011	Yangtze River, China, 1998	Bangla-desh, 1970	Yangtze River, China, 1990

worst oil spill

GULF WAR

During the Gulf War in 1991, Iraqi troops opened valves of oil wells in Kuwait, releasing more than 240 million gallons (908 million L) of oil into the Persian Gulf. At its worst, the spill measured 101 miles by 42 miles (163 km by 68 km) and was about 5 inches (13 cm) thick. Some of the oil eventually evaporated, another 1 million barrels were collected out of the water, and the rest washed ashore. Although much of the oil can no longer be seen, most of it remains, soaked into the deeper layers of sand along the coast. Amazingly, the wildlife that lives in these areas were not harmed as much as was initially feared. However, salt marsh areas without strong currents were hit the hardest, as oil collected there and killed off entire ecosystems.

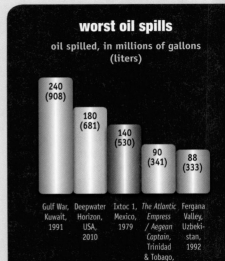

worst oil spills
oil spilled, in millions of gallons (liters)

240 (908)	180 (681)	140 (530)	90 (341)	88 (333)
Gulf War, Kuwait, 1991	Deepwater Horizon, USA, 2010	Ixtoc 1, Mexico, 1979	The Atlantic Empress / Aegean Captain, Trinidad & Tobago, 1979	Fergana Valley, Uzbekistan, 1992

most destructive tornado since 1900

JOPLIN, MISSOURI

On May 22, 2011, a category EF5 tornado ripped through Joplin, Missouri, and destroyed about 2,000 buildings, or 25 percent, of the small midwest town. The devastating storm caused damage totaling $2.8 billion and killed 161 people. The tornado measured up to a mile (1.6 km) wide, and was part of a large outbreak of storms during that week, which affected Arkansas, Kansas, and Oklahoma. A category-5 tornado on the Enhanced Fujita (EF) scale is the most intense, capable of producing winds greater than 200 miles (322 km) per hour. With more than 1,000 storms popping up across the country, 2011 was the deadliest year for tornadoes in fifty years.

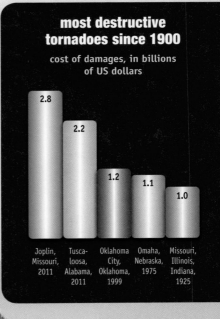

**most destructive
tornadoes since 1900**

cost of damages, in billions
of US dollars

Joplin, Missouri, 2011	Tusca- loosa, Alabama, 2011	Oklahoma City, Oklahoma, 1999	Omaha, Nebraska, 1975	Missouri, Illinois, Indiana, 1925
2.8	2.2	1.2	1.1	1.0

Devastation from
Hurricane Camille

most intense hurricanes since 1900

Hurricane Allen &
Hurricane Camille

Both Hurricane Allen and Hurricane
Camille were category 5 storms
with winds that gusted up to 190 miles
(306 km) per hour. Hurricane Camille made
landfall in the United States along the
mouth of the Mississippi River on August
17, 1969. The Gulf Coast and Virginia
sustained the most damage, and the
total storm damages cost $1.42 billion.
Hurricane Allen sustained its strongest
winds near Puerto Rico on August 5, 1980.
The storm traveled through the Caribbean,
Cuba, the Yucatan Peninsula, and the
south-central United States. The damages
totaled about $1 billion.

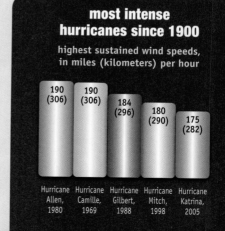

most intense
hurricanes since 1900

highest sustained wind speeds,
in miles (kilometers) per hour

Hurricane Allen, 1980	Hurricane Camille, 1969	Hurricane Gilbert, 1988	Hurricane Mitch, 1998	Hurricane Katrina, 2005
190 (306)	190 (306)	184 (296)	180 (290)	175 (282)

car Batteries

More than 96 percent of all used lead-acid car batteries in the United States are brought to recycling centers instead of being tossed in the trash. This is very good news for the environment because lead is a poisonous metal that can cause several illnesses if it seeps into soil or water that people use. About 97 percent of the lead found in a battery can be recycled. Other parts of the battery can be recycled as well, including sulfuric acid, which can be converted into sodium sulfate, used in fertilizers. Each year, Americans replace approximately 100 million car batteries.

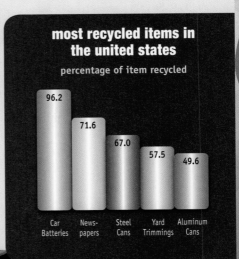

most recycled items in the united states

percentage of item recycled

Car Batteries	News-papers	Steel Cans	Yard Trimmings	Aluminum Cans
96.2	71.6	67.0	57.5	49.6

U.S.
records

alabama to wyoming

MAIL MOVERS

The US Postal Service delivers more mail to more addresses than any other post in the world—about 40 percent of the world's mail volume. They reach more than 150 million homes, businesses, and post office boxes. Averaging 6,400 pieces per minute, they process about 168 billion pieces of mail per year.

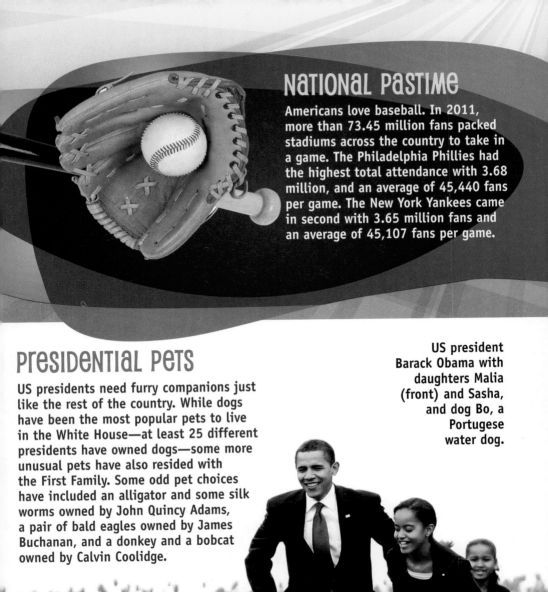

NATIONAL PASTIME

Americans love baseball. In 2011, more than 73.45 million fans packed stadiums across the country to take in a game. The Philadelphia Phillies had the highest total attendance with 3.68 million, and an average of 45,440 fans per game. The New York Yankees came in second with 3.65 million fans and an average of 45,107 fans per game.

PRESIDENTIAL PETS

US presidents need furry companions just like the rest of the country. While dogs have been the most popular pets to live in the White House—at least 25 different presidents have owned dogs—some more unusual pets have also resided with the First Family. Some odd pet choices have included an alligator and some silk worms owned by John Quincy Adams, a pair of bald eagles owned by James Buchanan, and a donkey and a bobcat owned by Calvin Coolidge.

US president Barack Obama with daughters Malia (front) and Sasha, and dog Bo, a Portugese water dog.

MONEY MAKERS

The US Mint makes way more coins than any other country. In fact, the United States makes coins for other countries as well. During 2011, they produced 4,938 million pennies, some 990 million nickels, more than 1,502 million dimes, and 391 million quarters. The Philadelphia Mint is the largest in the country at 5 square acres (2 sq ha).

PARKS FOR THE PEOPLE

The National Park System is made up of 397 different locations that are visited by more than 280 million people each year. The nation's parks are home to the world's longest cave system (Mammoth Cave), the highest point in North America (Mt. McKinley), and the lowest point in the western hemisphere (Death Valley).

Need For Speed

With more than 640 roller coasters, the United States has more scream machines than any other country in the world. The most common type by far is a sit-down coaster, followed by inverted and flying coasters. About 84 percent are made of steel.

Teeming With Tourists

Tourists love the United States—the top four of the world's most visited attractions are there! New York City's Times Square and Central Park are the top two, with 39.2 million and 38.0 million visitors respectively each year. Number three is Union Station in Washington, DC, with 37.0 million, followed by the Las Vegas Strip at 29.4 million visitors annually.

state with the oldest mardi gras celebration

ALABAMA

People in Mobile, Alabama, have been celebrating Mardi Gras since 1703, although they did not have an official parade event until 1831. After a brief hiatus during the Civil War, the celebrations started back up in 1866 and have been growing ever since. Today, some 100,000 people gather in Mobile to enjoy the 40 parades that take place during the two weeks that lead up to Mardi Gras. On the biggest day—Fat Tuesday— six parades wind through the downtown waterfront, with floats and costumed dancers. But at the stroke of midnight, the partying stops and plans for the next year begin.

united states' oldest mardi gras celebrations

number of years since celebration began*

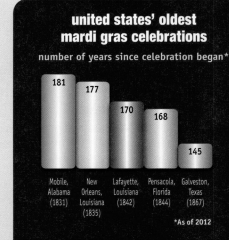

Mobile, Alabama (1831)	New Orleans, Louisiana (1835)	Lafayette, Louisiana (1842)	Pensacola, Florida (1844)	Galveston, Texas (1867)
181	177	170	168	145

*As of 2012

state with the largest national forest

alaska

The Tongass National Forest covers approximately 16,800,000 acres (6,798,900 ha) in southeast Alaska. That's about the same size as West Virginia. It is also home to the world's largest temperate rain forest. Some of the forest's trees are more than 700 years old. About 11,000 miles (17,703 km) of shoreline are inside the park. Some of the animals that live in the forest include bears, salmon, and wolves. The world's largest group of bald eagles also spend the fall and winter here on the Chilkat River.

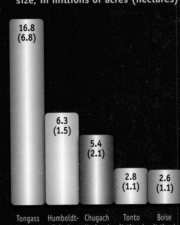

united states' largest national forests
size, in millions of acres (hectares)

16.8 (6.8)	6.3 (1.5)	5.4 (2.1)	2.8 (1.1)	2.6 (1.1)
Tongass National Forest, Alaska	Humboldt-Toiyabe National Forest, California/Nevada	Chugach National Forest, Alaska	Tonto National Forest, Arizona	Boise National Forest, Idaho

arizona

The Kitt Peak National Observatory is home to 26 different telescopes—24 optical telescopes and 2 radio telescopes. Located above the Sonora Desert, the site was chosen to house the collection of equipment because of its clear weather, low relative humidity, and steady atmosphere. Eight different astronomical research institutions maintain and operate the telescopes. The observatory is overseen by the National Optical Astronomy Observatories. One of the most prominent telescopes at Kitt Peak is the McMath-Pierce Solar Telescope, the second-largest solar telescope in the world.

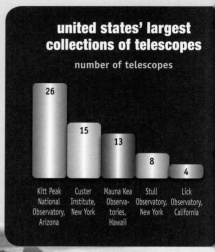

united states' largest collections of telescopes

number of telescopes

26	Kitt Peak National Observatory, Arizona
15	Custer Institute, New York
13	Mauna Kea Observatories, Hawaii
8	Stull Observatory, New York
4	Lick Observatory, California

state that grows the most rice

arkansas

Farmers in Arkansas produced 3.90 million tons (3.5 million t) of rice in 2011, which was more than 42 percent of all rice grown in the country. With that harvest, farmers could give every person in the United States 36 pounds (16 kg) of rice and still have a little left over. There are more than 1.19 million acres (484,004 ha) of rice planted across the state. Agriculture is a very important part of Arkansas's economy, employing more than 287,000 workers, or about 20 percent of the state's workforce.

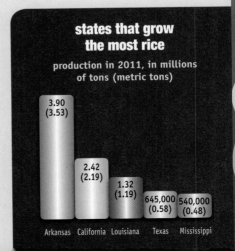

states that grow the most rice

production in 2011, in millions of tons (metric tons)

Arkansas	California	Louisiana	Texas	Mississippi
3.90 (3.53)	2.42 (2.19)	1.32 (1.19)	645,000 (0.58)	540,000 (0.48)

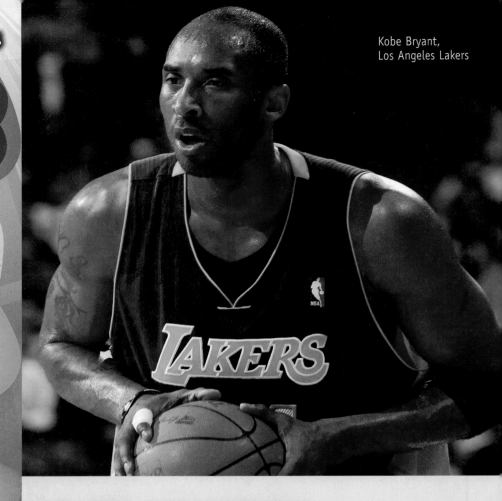

Kobe Bryant,
Los Angeles Lakers

state with the most pro sports teams

california

With 19 professional teams across the state, California leads the nation in sports franchises. The state's five baseball teams include the LA Angels, the LA Dodgers, the San Diego Padres, the Oakland A's, and the San Francisco Giants. California also has five basketball teams, including the NBA's LA Lakers, LA Clippers, Sacramento Kings, Golden State Warriors, and the WNBA's LA Sparks. The Anaheim Ducks, the LA Kings, and the San Jose Sharks are the hockey teams that call the state home. The NFL is represented in California by the Oakland Raiders, San Francisco 49ers, and the San Diego Chargers. Finally, the state's soccer teams include the San Jose Earthquakes, the LA Galaxy, and the Chivas USA.

states with the most pro sports teams

number of professional baseball, basketball, football, hockey, and soccer teams

California	New York	Texas	Florida	Pennsyl-vania
19	12	11	9	8

state with the tallest sand dunes

COLORADO

Star Dune, located in Great Sand Dunes National Park near Mosca, Colorado, is 750 feet (229 m) tall. That's almost five times taller than the Statue of Liberty! The park's dunes were formed from sand left behind by evaporated lakes. Wind picked up the sand and funneled it through the surrounding mountains until it collected in this low-lying region. Visitors to the park are allowed to ski, sled, or slide down the giant dunes; this works best after a light rain. Many animals also call this park home, including pika, marmots, black bears, and mountain lions.

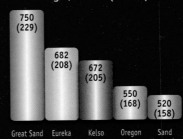

united states' tallest sand dunes

height, in feet (meters)

Great Sand Dunes, Colorado	Eureka Dunes, California	Kelso Dunes, California	Oregon Dunes, California	Sand Mountain, Nevada
750 (229)	682 (208)	672 (205)	550 (168)	520 (158)

state with the oldest amusement park

CONNECTICUT

Lake Compounce in Bristol, Connecticut, first opened as a picnic park in 1846. The park's first electric roller coaster, the Green Dragon, was introduced in 1914 and cost ten cents per ride. It was replaced by the Wildcat in 1927, and the wooden coaster still operates today. In 1996 the park got a $50 million upgrade, which included the thrilling new roller coaster Boulder Dash. It is the only coaster to built into a mountainside. Another $3.3 million was spent on upgrades in 2005, including an 800-foot (244 m) lazy river.

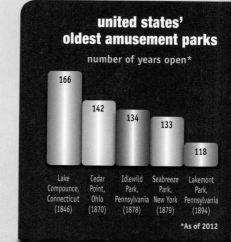

united states' oldest amusement parks

number of years open*

Lake Compounce, Connecticut (1846)	Cedar Point, Ohio (1870)	Idlewild Park, Pennsylvania (1878)	Seabreeze Park, New York (1879)	Lakemont Park, Pennsylvania (1894)
166	142	134	133	118

*As of 2012

state with the largest pumpkin-throwing contest

DeLaware

Each year approximately 20,000 people gather in Sussex County, Delaware, for the annual World Championship Punkin Chunkin. More than 70 teams compete during the three-day festival to see who can chuck their pumpkin the farthest. Each team constructs a machine that has a mechanical or compressed-air firing device—no explosives are allowed. The farthest a pumpkin has traveled during the championship is 4,483.5 feet (1,366 m), or the length of twelve football fields. The 2010 competition grossed more than $100,000, and more than $70,000 of it was donated to local scholarship funds. The first Punkin Chunkin competition was held in 1986.

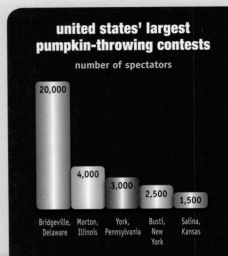

united states' largest pumpkin-throwing contests

number of spectators

Bridgeville, Delaware	Morton, Illinois	York, Pennsylvania	Busti, New York	Salina, Kansas
20,000	4,000	3,000	2,500	1,500

state with the most lightning strikes

FLORIDA

Southern Florida is known as the Lightning Capital of the United States, with 25.3 bolts occurring over each square mile (2.6 sq km)—the equivalent of ten city blocks—each year. Some 70 percent of all strikes occur between noon and 6:00 p.m., and the most dangerous months are July and August. Most lightning bolts measure 2 to 3 miles (5.2 to 7.8 km) long and can generate between 100 million and 1 billion volts of electricity. The air in a lightning bolt is heated to 50,000°F (27,760°C).

states with the most lightning strikes

annual bolts per square mile (2.6 sq km)

Florida	Louisiana	Mississippi	Alabama	South Carolina
25.3	20.3	18.0	15.9	14.6

state with the largest sports hall of fame

Georgia

The Georgia Sports Hall of Fame fills 43,000 square feet (3,995 sq m) with memorabilia from Georgia's most accomplished college, amateur, and professional athletes. Some 230,000 bricks, 245 tons (222 t) of steel, and 7,591 pounds (3,443 kg) of glass were used in its construction. The hall owns more than 3,000 artifacts and displays about 1,000 of them at a time. Some Hall of Famers include baseball legend Hank Aaron, Olympic basketball great Theresa Edwards, and Super Bowl I champion Bill Curry.

united states' largest sports halls of fame

area, in square feet (square meters)

Georgia Sports Hall of Fame	Virginia Sports Hall of Fame	Alabama Sports Hall of Fame	Mississippi Sports Hall of Fame	Kansas Sports Hall of Fame
43,000 (3,995)	35,000 (3,252)	33,000 (3,066)	21,542 (2,001)	21,000 (1,900)

state with the world's largest submillimeter wavelength telescope

Hawaii

Mauna Kea—located on the island of Hawaii—is home to the world's largest submillimeter wavelength telescope, with a diameter of 49 feet (15 m). The James Clerk Maxwell Telescope (JCMT) is used to study our solar system, interstellar dust and gas, and distant galaxies. Mauna Kea also houses one of the world's largest optical/infrared (Keck I and II) and dedicated infrared (UKIRT) telescopes in the world. Mauna Kea is an ideal spot for astronomy because the atmosphere above the dormant volcano is very dry with little cloud cover, and its distance from city lights ensures a clear night sky.

world's largest submillimeter wavelength telescopes

diameter of lens, in feet (meters)

49.0 (15.0)	34.0 (10.4)	32.8 (10.0)	32.8 (10.0)	32.8 (10.0)
James Clerk Maxwell Telescope (JCMT), Hawaii, USA	Caltech Submillimeter Observatory (CSO), Hawaii, USA	Atacama Submillimeter Telescope (ASTE), Chile	Heinrich Hertz Telescope (HHT), Arizona, USA	Submillimeter Telescope (SMT), Arizona, USA

state with the largest human-made geyser

IDAHO

The human-made geyser located in Soda Springs, Idaho, shoots water 150 feet (45.7 m) into the air. The geyser was created in November 1937 when people were searching for a hot water source for a thermal-heated swimming pool. The drill dug down about 315 feet (96 m) before it hit water. The pressure—created as water mixes with carbon dioxide gas—causes the water to shoot into the air. The Soda Springs geyser is now capped and controlled by a timer programmed to erupt every hour.

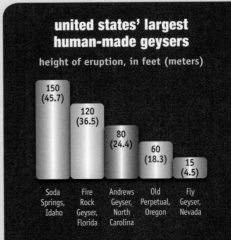

united states' largest human-made geysers

height of eruption, in feet (meters)

150 (45.7) — Soda Springs, Idaho

120 (36.5) — Fire Rock Geyser, Florida

80 (24.4) — Andrews Geyser, North Carolina

60 (18.3) — Old Perpetual, Oregon

15 (4.5) — Fly Geyser, Nevada

state with the tallest building

ILLINOIS

The Willis Tower in Chicago, Illinois, is the tallest building in the western hemisphere at 1,451 feet (442 m). It is the ninth-tallest building in the world. Rising 110 stories above the pavement, the building offers about 3.8 million square feet (353,031 sq m) of retail and office space. The building, which was completed in 1973 as the Sears Tower, cost more than $150 million to build. It has a sky deck that offers visitors a view from the 103rd floor. The Willis Tower will lose the tallest building title, however, when the Freedom Tower in New York City is completed at a height of 1,776 feet (541 m).

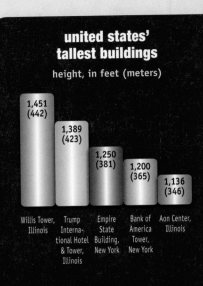

united states' tallest buildings

height, in feet (meters)

Willis Tower, Illinois	Trump International Hotel & Tower, Illinois	Empire State Building, New York	Bank of America Tower, New York	Aon Center, Illinois
1,451 (442)	1,389 (423)	1,250 (381)	1,200 (365)	1,136 (346)

state with the largest half marathon

INDIANA

Cars aren't the only things racing in Indianapolis, Indiana. Each May some 35,000 runners take part in the OneAmerica 500 Festival Mini-Marathon. This makes the Mini-Marathon the nation's largest half marathon and the nation's eighth-longest road race. The 13.1-mile (21.1 km) race winds through downtown and includes a lap along the Indianapolis Motor Speedway oval. About 100 musical groups entertain the runners as they complete the course. A giant pasta dinner and after-race party await the runners at the end of the day. The Mini-Marathon is part of a weekend celebration that centers around the Indianapolis 500 auto race.

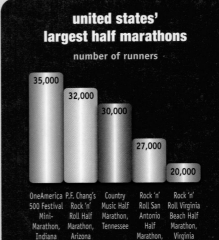

united states' largest half marathons
number of runners

35,000	32,000	30,000	27,000	20,000
OneAmerica 500 Festival Mini-Marathon, Indiana	P.F. Chang's Rock 'n' Roll Half Marathon, Arizona	Country Music Half Marathon, Tennessee	Rock 'n' Roll San Antonio Half Marathon, Texas	Rock 'n' Roll Virginia Beach Half Marathon, Virginia

state with the highest egg production

iowa

Iowa tops all other states in the country in egg production, turning out more than 14.4 billion eggs per year. That's enough to give every person in the United States about three and a half dozen eggs each! That's a good thing, because each person in America eats about 248 eggs per year. The state has 57 million laying hens, and each is capable of laying about 254 eggs a year. These hungry hens eat about 57 million bushels of corn and 28.5 million bushels of soybeans annually. In addition to selling the eggs as they are, Iowa's processing plants turn them into frozen, liquid, dried, or specialty egg products.

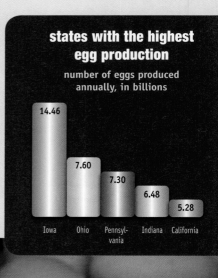

states with the highest egg production

number of eggs produced annually, in billions

Iowa	Ohio	Pennsylvania	Indiana	California
14.46	7.60	7.30	6.48	5.28

state with the windiest city

kansas

According to average annual wind speeds collected by the National Climatic Data Center, Dodge City, Kansas, is the windiest city in the United States, with an average wind speed of 13.9 miles (22.3 km) per hour. Located in Ford County, the city borders the Santa Fe Trail and is rich in history. The city was founded in 1872 and had a reputation as a tough cowboy town. With help from legendary sheriffs like Wyatt Earp, order was established and the town grew steadily. Today, tourists come to learn about the area's history.

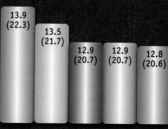

united states' windiest cities

average wind speed, in miles (kilometers) per hour

Dodge City, Kansas	Amarillo, Texas	Rochester, Minnesota	Cheyenne, Wyoming	Kahului, Hawaii
13.9 (22.3)	13.5 (21.7)	12.9 (20.7)	12.9 (20.7)	12.8 (20.6)

state with the most popular horse race

KENTUCKY

Each year, the Kentucky Derby draws more than 164,858 people who gather to watch "the most exciting two minutes in sports." The race is run at Churchill Downs in Louisville, on a dirt track that measures 1.25 miles (2 km) long. The thoroughbred horses must be three years old to race, and the winner nabs a $2 million purse. The winning horse is covered in a blanket of 554 red roses, which gave the race the nickname "The Run for the Roses." The fastest horse to complete the race was Secretariat in 1973, with a time of 1:59:40.

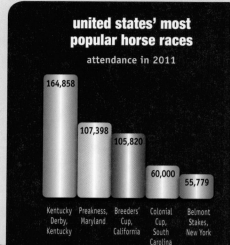

united states' most popular horse races
attendance in 2011

Kentucky Derby, Kentucky	Preakness, Maryland	Breeders' Cup, California	Colonial Cup, South Carolina	Belmont Stakes, New York
164,858	107,398	105,820	60,000	55,779

Secretariat

GATOR XING
NEXT 1/2 MILE

state with the largest alligator population

LOUISIANA

There are approximately 2 million alligators living in Louisiana. About 1.5 million alligators live in the wild, and another half million are raised on farms. In 1986, Louisiana began an alligator ranching business, which encourages farmers to raise thousands of the reptiles each year. The farmers must return some alligators to the wild, but they are allowed to sell the rest for profit. The released alligators have an excellent chance of thriving in the wild because they have been well fed and are a good size. Although alligators can be found in the state's bayous, swamps, and ponds, most live in Louisiana's 3 million acres (1.2 million ha) of coastal marshland.

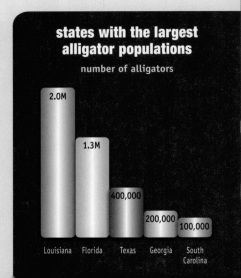

states with the largest alligator populations

number of alligators

Louisiana	Florida	Texas	Georgia	South Carolina
2.0M	1.3M	400,000	200,000	100,000

state with the oldest state fair

Maine

The first Skowhegan State Fair took place in 1819—a year before Maine officially became a state! The fair took place in January, and hundreds of people came despite harsh weather. Originally sponsored by the Somerset Central Agricultural Society, the fair name became official in 1842. State fairs were very important in the 1800s. With no agricultural colleges in existence, fairs became the best way for farmers to learn about new agricultural methods and equipment. Today, the Skowhegan State Fair features more than 7,000 exhibitors who compete for prize money totaling more than $200,000. The fair also includes a demolition derby, a children's barnyard, concerts, livestock exhibits, and arts and crafts.

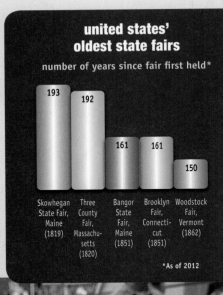

united states' oldest state fairs

number of years since fair first held*

193	192	161	161	150
Skowhegan State Fair, Maine (1819)	Three County Fair, Massachusetts (1820)	Bangor State Fair, Maine (1851)	Brooklyn Fair, Connecticut (1851)	Woodstock Fair, Vermont (1862)

*As of 2012

College Park Aviation Museum

state with the oldest airport

MARYLAND

The Wright brothers founded College Park Airport in 1909 to teach army officers how to fly, and it has been in operation ever since. The airport is now owned by the Maryland-National Capital Park and Planning Commission and is on the Register of Historic Places. Many aviation "firsts" occurred at this airport, such as the first woman passenger in the United States (1909), the first test of a bomb-dropping device (1911), and the first US airmail service (1918). The College Park Aviation Museum is located on its grounds, and it exhibits aviation memorabilia.

united states' oldest airports

number of years open*

103	101	92	91	88
College Park Airport, Maryland (1909)	Robertson Airport, Connecticut (1911)	Hartness State Airport, Vermont (1920)	Middlesboro-Bell County Airport, Kentucky (1921)	Page Field, Florida (1924)

*As of 2012

massachusetts

Fenway Park opened its doors to Massachusetts baseball fans on April 20, 1912. The Boston Red Sox—the park's home team—won the World Series that year. The park celebrated in 2004 when the Sox won the World Series again. The park is also the home of the Green Monster—a giant 37-foot (11.3 m) wall with an additional 23-foot (7 m) screen that has plagued home-run hitters since the park first opened. The park's unique dimensions were not intended to prevent home runs, however; they were meant to keep nonpaying fans outside. A seat out in the right-field bleachers is painted red to mark where the longest measurable home run hit inside the park landed. It measured 502 feet (153 m) and was hit by Ted Williams in 1946. Some of the other baseball legends who played at Fenway include Cy Young, Babe Ruth, Jimmie Fox, and Carlton Fisk.

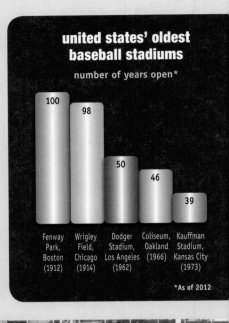

united states' oldest baseball stadiums

number of years open*

Stadium	Years Open
Fenway Park, Boston (1912)	100
Wrigley Field, Chicago (1914)	98
Dodger Stadium, Los Angeles (1962)	50
Coliseum, Oakland (1966)	46
Kauffman Stadium, Kansas City (1973)	39

*As of 2012

state with the largest stadium

MICHIGAN

Michigan Stadium—also known as the Big House—is the home of the University of Michigan Wolverines, and can hold 109,901 football fans during the home games. The stadium was constructed in 1927 using 440 tons (399 t) of reinforcing steel and 31,000 square feet (2,880 sq m) of wire mesh to create a 82,000-seat venue. After several renovations, the stadium reached its current seating capacity in 2010. The most recent additions include luxury boxes and club seating. Since its inaugural game, Michigan Stadium has hosted more than 35 million fans.

united states' largest stadiums

seating capacity

Michigan Stadium, Michigan	Beaver Stadium, Pennsyl-vania	Neyland Stadium, Tennessee	Ohio Stadium, Ohio	Bryant-Denny Stadium, Alabama
109,901	107,282	102,455	102,329	101,821

state with the largest indoor amusement park

MINNESOTA

Nickelodeon Universe is located inside the Mall of America in Bloomington, Minnesota, and covers 7 acres (2.8 ha). The park offers 30 rides, including the Xcel Energy Log Chute, SpongeBob SquarePants Rock Bottom Plunge, Splat-O-Sphere, Skyscraper Ferris wheel, Timber Twister roller coaster, Mighty Axe, and Avatar Airbender. Some of the other attractions at the park are a rock-climbing wall, petting zoo, and game arcade. Kids can also meet Dora, Diego, Blue, and SpongeBob.

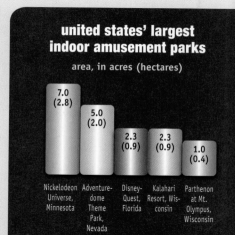

united states' largest indoor amusement parks

area, in acres (hectares)

Nickelodeon Universe, Minnesota	Adventure-dome Theme Park, Nevada	Disney-Quest, Florida	Kalahari Resort, Wisconsin	Parthenon at Mt. Olympus, Wisconsin
7.0 (2.8)	5.0 (2.0)	2.3 (0.9)	2.3 (0.9)	1.0 (0.4)

state with the most catfish

MISSISSIPPI

Mississippi sold $215 million in catfish in 2011. There are about 388 million catfish in Mississippi—more than 60 percent of the world's farm-raised supply. That's almost enough to give every person in the state about 132 fish each. There are about 80,200 water acres (32,000 ha) used to farm catfish in Mississippi. The state's residents are quite proud of their successful fish industry and celebrate at the World Catfish Festival in Belzoni.

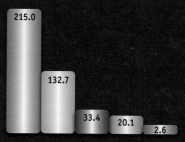

states with the most catfish
total sales in 2011, in millions

Mississippi	Alabama	Arkansas	Texas	Louisiana
215.0	132.7	33.4	20.1	2.6

state with the largest outdoor theater

MISSOURI

The Municipal Theatre in St. Louis, Missouri—affectionately known as the Muny—is the nation's largest outdoor theater, with 80,000 square feet (7,432 sq m) and 11,500 seats—about the same size as a regulation soccer field. Amazingly, construction for the giant theater was completed in just 42 days at a cost of $10,000. The theater opened in 1917 with a production of Verdi's *Aïda*, and the best seats cost only $1. The Muny offers classic Broadway shows each summer, with past productions including *The King and I*, *The Wizard of Oz*, and *Oliver!* The last nine rows of the theater are always held as free seats for the public, just as they have been since the Muny opened.

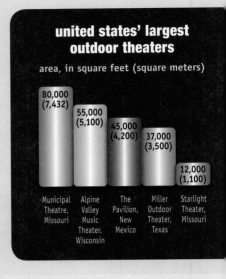

united states' largest outdoor theaters

area, in square feet (square meters)

Municipal Theatre, Missouri	Alpine Valley Music Theater, Wisconsin	The Pavilion, New Mexico	Miller Outdoor Theater, Texas	Starlight Theater, Missouri
80,000 (7,432)	55,000 (5,100)	45,000 (4,200)	37,000 (3,500)	12,000 (1,100)

state with the largest bighorn sheep population

MONTANA

With a population of about 5,700 bighorn sheep, Montana has more of these wild endangered mammals than any other state. The population has quadrupled in the last 60 years. Many of Montana's bighorn sheep live in an area known as the Rocky Mountain Front—a 100-mile (160.9-km) area that stretches from Glacier National Park to the town of Lincoln. A ram's horns can weigh up to 30 pounds (13.6 kg)—more than all of the bones in its body. Rams use these giant horns when they butt heads with a rival, and can hit each other at up to 20 miles (32.2 km) per hour.

states with the largest bighorn sheep populations

number of sheep

Montana	Nevada	Utah	California	Texas
5,700	5,000	4,900	4,300	1,115

state with the world's largest indoor rain forest

NEBRASKA

At 123,000 square feet (11,427 sq m), the Lied Jungle at the Henry Doorly Zoo in Omaha is the world's largest indoor rain forest. The eight-story-tall building houses rain-forest exhibits from Asia, Africa, and South America that include plants, trees, caves, cliffs, bridges, and waterfalls. Some ninety different animals species live in these exhibits, including gibbons, small-clawed otters, spider monkeys, pygmy hippos, tapirs, and many birds and reptiles. Some exotic tree species include chocolate, allspice, African sausage, and black pepper. The giant roof lets in sunlight to promote natural growth. The jungle opened in 1992 and cost $15 million to create.

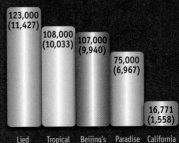

world's largest indoor rain forests

size in square feet (square meters)

123,000 (11,427)	Lied Jungle, Nebraska
108,000 (10,033)	Tropical Islands, Germany
107,000 (9,940)	Beijing's National Hotel, China
75,000 (6,967)	Paradise Earth, Arizona
16,771 (1,558)	California Academy of Sciences, California

state with the largest glass sculpture

NEVADA

Fiori di Como—the breathtaking chandelier at the Bellagio Hotel in Las Vegas, Nevada—measures 65.7 feet by 29.5 feet (20 m by 9 m). Created by Dale Chihuly, the handblown glass chandelier consists of more than 2,000 discs of colored glass. Each disc is about 18 inches (45.7 cm) wide and hangs about 20 feet (6.1 m) overhead. Together, these colorful discs look like a giant field of flowers. The chandelier required about 10,000 pounds (4,536 kg) of steel and 40,000 pounds (18,144 kg) of handblown glass. The sculpture's name translates to "Flowers of Como." The Bellagio was modeled after a hotel on Lake Como in Italy.

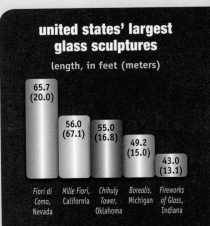

united states' largest glass sculptures
length, in feet (meters)

Sculpture	Length in feet (meters)
Fiori di Como, Nevada	65.7 (20.0)
Mille Fiori, California	56.0 (67.1)
Chihuly Tower, Oklahoma	55.0 (16.8)
Borealis, Michigan	49.2 (15.0)
Fireworks of Glass, Indiana	43.0 (13.1)

state with the oldest lottery

NEW HAMPSHIRE

New Hampshire was the first state to establish a legal lottery system when it sold its first ticket in 1964. The lottery was originally established to raise money for charitable causes throughout the state. Since it began, the New Hampshire Lottery has seen more than $4.1 billion in sales and other earnings—about $2.7 billion was paid out as prize money, and about $1.3 billion has gone to fund education in the state. The main in-state lottery in New Hampshire is called the Weekly Grand, but residents also participate in several multistate lotteries as well.

states with the oldest lotteries

number of years in existence*

New Hampshire	New York	New Jersey	Connecti-cut	Pennsyl-vania
48	45	42	41	41

*As of 2012

state with the world's longest boardwalk

NEW JERSEY

The famous boardwalk in Atlantic City, New Jersey, stretches for 4 miles (6.4 km) along the beach. Combined with the adjoining boardwalk in Ventnor, the length increases to just under 6 miles (9.7 km). The 60-foot (18 m) wide boardwalk opened on June 26, 1870. It was the first boardwalk built in the United States, and was designed to keep sand out of the tourists' shoes. Today, the boardwalk is filled with amusement parks, shops, restaurants, and hotels. The boardwalk recently received a $100 million face-lift, which included new roofs, signs, and storefronts for surrounding buildings. About 37 million people take a stroll along the walk each year.

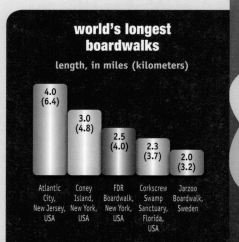

world's longest boardwalks

length, in miles (kilometers)

Atlantic City, New Jersey, USA	Coney Island, New York, USA	FDR Boardwalk, New York, USA	Corkscrew Swamp Sanctuary, Florida, USA	Jarzoo Boardwalk, Sweden
4.0 (6.4)	3.0 (4.8)	2.5 (4.0)	2.3 (3.7)	2.0 (3.2)

state with the world's largest balloon festival

New Mexico

During the 2011 Kodak Albuquerque International Balloon Fiesta in New Mexico, approximately 700 hot-air and gas-filled balloons sailed across the sky. Held each October, the fiesta draws more than 800,000 spectators. This event attracts balloons from around the world, and is often seen in more than 50 countries. The festival takes place in the 200-acre (81 ha) Balloon Fiesta State Park. The Balloon Fiesta has also hosted some prestigious balloon races, including the Gordon Bennett Cup (1993), the World Gas Balloon Championship (1994), and the America's Challenge Gas Balloon Race (2006).

world's largest balloon festivals

approximate number of balloons

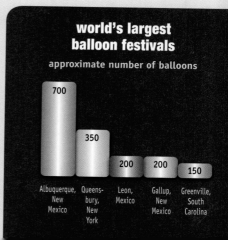

700	350	200	200	150
Albuquerque, New Mexico	Queensbury, New York	Leon, Mexico	Gallup, New Mexico	Greenville, South Carolina

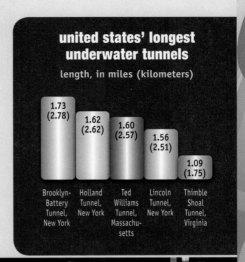

state with the longest underwater tunnel

NEW YORK

The Brooklyn-Battery Tunnel in New York measures 1.73 miles (2.78 km) long, making it the longest underwater tunnel in North America and the longest continuous underwater vehicular tunnel in the world. The tunnel passes under the East River and connects Battery Park in Manhattan with the Red Hook section of Brooklyn. It took 13,900 tons (12,609 t) of steel, about 205,000 cubic yards (156,700 cu m) of concrete, approximately 1,871 miles (3,011 km) of electrical wire, some 883,391 bolts, and 799,000 wall and ceiling tiles to build the tunnel. Completed in 1950, the $90-million tunnel carries about 60,000 vehicles a day.

united states' longest underwater tunnels

length, in miles (kilometers)

Tunnel	Length
Brooklyn-Battery Tunnel, New York	1.73 (2.78)
Holland Tunnel, New York	1.62 (2.62)
Ted Williams Tunnel, Massachusetts	1.60 (2.57)
Lincoln Tunnel, New York	1.56 (2.51)
Thimble Shoal Tunnel, Virginia	1.09 (1.75)

state that grows the most sweet potatoes

NORTH CAROLINA

North Carolina leads the country in sweet potato production, growing about 1.21 billion pounds (548.8 kg) each year. This accounts for more than 41 percent of the nation's sweet potato production. Farmers plant about 55,000 acres (22,257 ha) of sweet potato plants annually. In fact, the sweet potato is the official state vegetable of North Carolina. Oddly enough, these sweet veggies aren't really potatoes at all. Sweet potatoes are root plants— not tubers—and are actually part of the morning glory family.

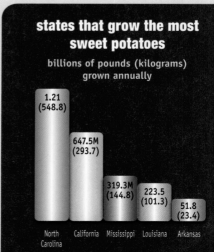

states that grow the most sweet potatoes

billions of pounds (kilograms) grown annually

North Carolina	California	Mississippi	Louisiana	Arkansas
1.21 (548.8)	647.5M (293.7)	319.3M (144.8)	223.5 (101.3)	51.8 (23.4)

state with the tallest metal sculpture

NORTH DaKOTa

In August 2001, Gary Greff created a 110-foot (33.5 m) tall metal sculpture along the stretch of road between Gladstone and Regent, North Dakota. That's the height of an 11-story building! The 154-foot (46.9 m) wide sculpture is called *Geese in Flight*, and shows Canada geese traveling across the prairie. Greff has created several other towering sculptures nearby, and the road has become known as the Enchanted Highway. He created these sculptures to attract tourists to the area and to support his hometown. He relies only on donations to finance his work.

united states' tallest metal sculptures

height, in feet (meters)

110 (33.5)	75 (22.9)	70 (21.3)	60 (18.3)	60 (18.3)
Geese in Flight, North Dakota	Deer Crossing, North Dakota	Bass Fish, North Dakota	Grasshopper Delight, North Dakota	Needle Tower, Oregon

state with the world's largest twins gathering

OHIO

Each August, the town of Twinsburg, Ohio, hosts more than 3,400 twins at its annual Twins Day Festival. Both identical and fraternal twins from around the world participate, and many dress alike. The twins take part in games and contests, such as the oldest identical twins and the twins with the widest combined smile. There is also a Double Take parade, which is nationally televised. There are special twin programs for all age groups, since twins from ages 90 years to just 11 days old have attended. The event began in 1976 in honor of Aaron and Moses Wilcox, twin brothers who inspired the city to adopt its name in 1817.

world's largest twins gatherings

number of attendees

Twins Day Festival, Ohio, USA	Twins Weekend, Canada	"Deux et plus" Gathering, France	Twins Plus Festival, Australia	Montreal Canada Twins Festival, Canada
3,400	2,500	2,000	1,400	1,000

state with the world's longest multiple-arch dam

OKLAHOMA

With a length of 6,565 feet (2,001 m), the Pensacola Dam in Oklahoma is the world's longest multiple-arch dam. Built in 1940, the dam is located on the Grand River and contains the Grand Lake o' the Cherokees— one of the largest reservoirs in the country, with 46,500 surface acres (18,818 ha) of water. The dam stands 145 feet (44 m) high. It was made out of 535,000 cubic yards of concrete, some 655,000 barrels of cement, another 10 million pounds (4.5 million kg) of structural steel, and 75,000 pounds (340,194 kg) of copper. The dam cost $27 million to complete.

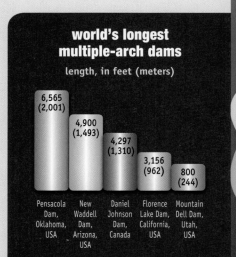

world's longest multiple-arch dams

length, in feet (meters)

Pensacola Dam, Oklahoma, USA	6,565 (2,001)
New Waddell Dam, Arizona, USA	4,900 (1,493)
Daniel Johnson Dam, Canada	4,297 (1,310)
Florence Lake Dam, California, USA	3,156 (962)
Mountain Dell Dam, Utah, USA	800 (244)

state with the deepest lake

OreGON

At a depth of 1,932 feet (589 m), Crater Lake in southern Oregon partially fills the remains of an old volcanic basin. The crater was formed almost 7,700 years ago when Mount Mazama erupted and then collapsed. The lake averages about 5 miles (8 km) in diameter. Crater Lake National Park—the nation's fifth-oldest park—surrounds the majestic lake and measures 249 square miles (645 sq km). The area's large snowfalls average 530 inches (1,346 cm) a year, and supply Crater Lake with its water. In addition to being the United States' deepest lake, it's also the eighth-deepest lake in the world.

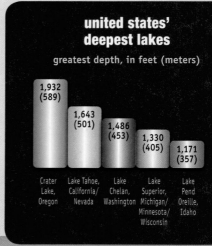

united states' deepest lakes

greatest depth, in feet (meters)

1,932 (589)	1,643 (501)	1,486 (453)	1,330 (405)	1,171 (357)
Crater Lake, Oregon	Lake Tahoe, California/ Nevada	Lake Chelan, Washington	Lake Superior, Michigan/ Minnesota/ Wisconsin	Lake Pend Oreille, Idaho

state with the oldest operating drive-in theater

PENNSYLVANIA

Shankweiler's Drive-in Theatre opened in 1934. It was the country's second drive-in theater, and is the oldest one still operating today. Located in Orefield, Pennsylvania, the single-screen theater can accommodate 320 cars. Approximately 90 percent of the theater's guests are children. Although they originally used sound boxes located beside the cars, today's patrons can tune into a special radio station to hear the movies' music and dialogue. Shankweiler's is open from April to September.

united states' oldest operating drive-in theaters
number of years open*

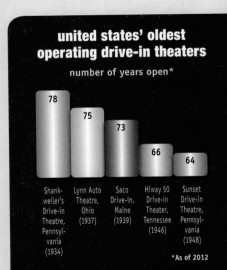

Shank-weiler's Drive-in Theatre, Pennsyl-vania (1934)	Lynn Auto Theatre, Ohio (1937)	Saco Drive-in, Maine (1939)	Hiway 50 Drive-in Theater, Tennessee (1946)	Sunset Drive-in Theatre, Pennsyl-vania (1948)
78	75	73	66	64

*As of 2012

state with the oldest temple

rHODe ISLanD

The Touro Synagogue was dedicated during Hanukkah in December 1763 and is the oldest temple in the United States. Located in Newport, Rhode Island, the temple was designed by famous architect Peter Harrison and took four years to complete. In addition to serving as a symbol of religious freedom, the temple played another part in the country's history. When the British captured Newport in 1776, the temple briefly became a British hospital. Then, in 1781, George Washington met General Lafayette there to plan the final battles of the Revolution.

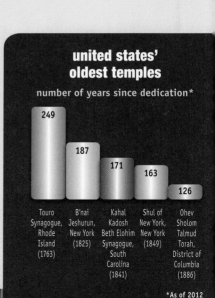

united states' oldest temples

number of years since dedication*

249	187	171	163	126
Touro Synagogue, Rhode Island (1763)	B'nai Jeshurun, New York (1825)	Kahal Kadosh Beth Elohim Synagogue, South Carolina (1841)	Shul of New York, New York (1849)	Ohev Sholom Talmud Torah, District of Columbia (1886)

*As of 2012

state with the oldest museum
SOUTH CaroLiNa

The Charleston Museum in Charleston, South Carolina, was founded in 1773— three years before the Declaration of Independence was signed. The museum was founded to preserve the culture and history of the southern town and the surrounding area, and opened its doors to the public in 1824. Some of the exhibits in the museum include furniture, silver, and art made in the area, as well as fossils of local birds and animals. Two historic houses, which were built between 1772 and 1803, are also run by the museum. Visitors can tour these homes to learn about the state's early architecture.

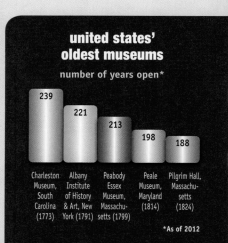

united states' oldest museums
number of years open*

Charleston Museum, South Carolina (1773)	Albany Institute of History & Art, New York (1791)	Peabody Essex Museum, Massachu- setts (1799)	Peale Museum, Maryland (1814)	Pilgrim Hall, Massachu- setts (1824)
239	221	213	198	188

*As of 2012

state with the largest petrified wood collection

SOUTH DAKOTA

Lemmon's Petrified Wood Park in South Dakota is home to 30 acres (12.1 ha) of petrified wood. It covers an entire city block in downtown Lemmon. It was built between 1930 and 1932 when locals collected petrified wood from the area and constructed displays. One structure in the park—known as the Castle—weighs more than 300 tons (272 t) and is made partly from petrified wood and partly of petrified dinosaur and mammoth bones. Other exhibits include a wishing well, a waterfall, the Lemmon Pioneer Museum, and hundreds of pile sculptures.

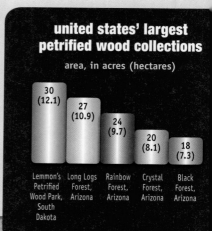

united states' largest petrified wood collections

area, in acres (hectares)

Lemmon's Petrified Wood Park, South Dakota	Long Logs Forest, Arizona	Rainbow Forest, Arizona	Crystal Forest, Arizona	Black Forest, Arizona
30 (12.1)	27 (10.9)	24 (9.7)	20 (8.1)	18 (7.3)

state with the world's largest freshwater aquarium

TENNESSEE

The Tennessee Aquarium in Chattanooga is an impressive 130,000 square feet (12,077 sq m), making it the largest freshwater aquarium in the world. The $45 million building holds a total of 400,000 gallons (1,514,165 L) of water. In addition, the aquarium features a 60,000-square-foot (5,574 sq m) building dedicated to the ocean and the creatures that live there. Permanent features in the aquarium include a discovery hall and an environmental learning lab. Some of the aquarium's 12,000 animals include baby alligators, paddlefish, lake sturgeon, sea dragons, and pipefish. And to feed all of these creatures, the aquarium goes through 12,000 crickets, 33,300 worms, and 1,200 pounds (545 kg) of seafood each month!

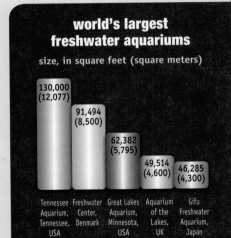

world's largest freshwater aquariums

size, in square feet (square meters)

130,000 (12,077)	91,494 (8,500)	62,382 (5,795)	49,514 (4,600)	46,285 (4,300)
Tennessee Aquarium, Tennessee, USA	Freshwater Center, Denmark	Great Lakes Aquarium, Minnesota, USA	Aquarium of the Lakes, UK	Gifu Freshwater Aquarium, Japan

state with the biggest ferris wheel

Texas

The State Fair of Texas boasts the nation's largest Ferris wheel. Called the Texas Star, this colossal wheel measures 212 feet (64.6 m) high. That's taller than a 20-story building! The Texas Star was built in Italy and shipped to Texas for its debut at the 1986 fair. Located in the 277-acre (112 ha) Fair Park, the Texas Star is just one of the 70 rides featured at the fair. The three-week-long State Fair of Texas is the biggest state fair in the country and brings in about $350 million in revenue annually. It is held in the fall, and the giant Ferris wheel is not the only grand-scale item there. Big Tex, a 52-foot (15.9 m) tall cowboy, is the fair's mascot and the tallest cowboy in the United States.

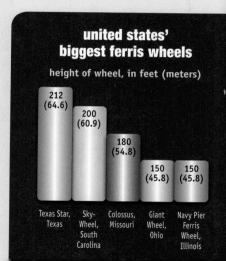

united states' biggest ferris wheels

height of wheel, in feet (meters)

Texas Star, Texas	Sky-Wheel, South Carolina	Colossus, Missouri	Giant Wheel, Ohio	Navy Pier Ferris Wheel, Illinois
212 (64.6)	200 (60.9)	180 (54.8)	150 (45.8)	150 (45.8)

state with the largest dinosaur collection

UTaH

The Museum of Ancient Life at the Thanksgiving Point Institute in Lehi, Utah, has the largest dinosaur collection in the country with 60 complete skeletons on display. Guests are even invited to touch some of the real fossils, bones, and eggs that they are looking at. There are about 50 interactive displays throughout the Museum of Ancient Life. Guests touring the museum can also observe a working paleontology lab. The museum, which opened in June 2000, holds a sleepover once a month for kids to go on a behind-the-scenes tour.

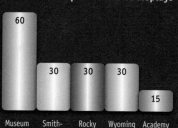

united states' largest dinosaur collections

number of complete skeletal displays

Museum of Ancient Life, Utah	Smithsonian Museum of Natural History, District of Columbia	Rocky Mountain Dinosaur Research Center, Colorado	Wyoming Dinosaur Center, Wyoming	Academy of Natural Sciences, Pennsylvania
60	30	30	30	15

state that produces the most maple syrup

VERMONT

Maple syrup production in Vermont totaled more than 1.14 billion gallons (4,315,369 L) in 2011 and accounted for about 41 percent of the United States' total yield that year. There are approximately 3.2 million tree taps used by the state's 2,000 maple syrup producers, and the annual production generates almost $13.1 million. It takes about five tree taps to collect enough maple sap—approximately 40 gallons (151.4 L)—to produce just 1 gallon (3.79 L) of syrup. Vermont maple syrup is also made into maple sugar, maple cream, and maple candies.

states that produce the most maple syrup

production, in gallons (liters)

Vermont	New York	Maine	Wisconsin	New Hamp-shire
1.14B (4,315,369)	564,000 (2,134,972)	360,000 (1,362,748)	155,000 (586,738)	128,000 (484,532)

state with the largest office building

VIRGINIA

The Pentagon Building in Arlington, Virginia, measures 6,636,360 square feet (616,538 sq m) and covers 583 acres (236 ha). In fact, the US Capitol can fit inside the building five times! Although the Pentagon contains 17.5 miles (28.2 km) of hallways, the design of the building allows people to reach any destination in about seven minutes. The Pentagon is almost like a small city, employing about 23,000 people. About 200,000 phone calls are made there daily, and the internal post office handles an average of 1.2 million pieces of mail each month.

united states' largest office buildings

size, in millions of square feet (square meters)

Pentagon, Virginia	Willis Tower, Illinois	Aon Center, Illinois	Empire State Building, New York	Equitable Building, New York
6.63 (616,538)	3.80 (353,091)	2.50 (232,000)	2.10 (195,000)	1.24 (115,200)

state with the longest train tunnel

WASHINGTON

The Cascade Tunnel runs through the Cascade Mountains in central Washington and measures 7.8 miles (12.6 km) long. The tunnel connects the towns of Berne and Scenic. It was built by the Great Northern Railway in 1929 to replace the original tunnel, which was built at an elevation frequently hit with snowslides. To help cool the trains' diesel engines and remove fumes, the tunnel is equipped with huge fans that blow air while and after a train passes.

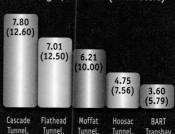

united states' longest train tunnels

length, in miles (kilometers)

Cascade Tunnel, Washington	Flathead Tunnel, Missouri	Moffat Tunnel, Colorado	Hoosac Tunnel, Massachusetts	BART Transbay Tube, California
7.80 (12.60)	7.01 (12.50)	6.21 (10.00)	4.75 (7.56)	3.60 (5.79)

CASCADE TUNNEL
7.8 MILES LONG   ELEVATION 2,247 FEET
41,152 FEET LONG   COMPLETED 1928

state with the longest steel arch bridge

WEST VIRGINIA

With a main span of 1,700 feet (518 m) and a weight of about 88 million pounds (40 million kg), the New River Gorge Bridge in Fayetteville, West Virginia, is the longest and largest steel arch bridge in the United States. It is approximately 875 feet (267 m) above the New River and is the second-highest bridge in the country. After three years of construction, the bridge was completed in 1977. The $37 million structure is the focus of Bridge Day—a statewide annual festival that is one of the largest extreme sports events in the United States, drawing hundreds of BASE jumpers and thousands of spectators.

united states' longest steel arch bridges

length of main span, in feet (meters)

Bridge	Length
New River Gorge Bridge, West Virginia	1,700 (518)
Bayonne Bridge, New Jersey	1,675 (511)
Fremont Bridge, Oregon	1,255 (383)
Roosevelt Lake Bridge, Arizona	1,080 (329)
Hell Gate Bridge, New York	1,038 (316)

state with the largest water park

WISCONSIN

Noah's Ark in Wisconsin Dells, Wisconsin, sprawls for 70 acres (28.4 ha) and includes 49 waterslides. One of the most popular—Dark Voyage—takes visitors on a twisting rapids ride in the dark. The ride can pump 8,000 gallons (30,283 L) of water a minute. Visitors can also enjoy two wave pools, two mile-long "endless" rivers, and four children's play areas. It takes 5 million gallons (19 million L) of water—the equivalent of more than 14 Olympic-size swimming pools—to fill all the pools and operate the 3 miles (4.8 km) of waterslides. Noah's Ark also boasts the country's longest water coaster (Black Anaconda), the world's longest bowl ride (Time Warp), and the world's only 4-D drive-in theater.

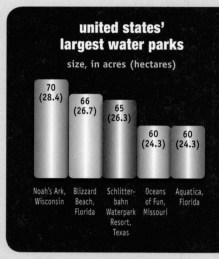

united states' largest water parks

size, in acres (hectares)

70 (28.4)	66 (26.7)	65 (26.3)	60 (24.3)	60 (24.3)
Noah's Ark, Wisconsin	Blizzard Beach, Florida	Schlitter-bahn Waterpark Resort, Texas	Oceans of Fun, Missouri	Aquatica, Florida

state with the largest outdoor rodeo

WYOMING

Cheyenne Frontier Days in Cheyenne, Wyoming, brings more than 252,000 spectators to the city during the last full week of July. The festival is not only the largest rodeo in the world but also the oldest continually running. Some 1,800 cowboys and cowgirls compete for the $1 million in prize money. Besides the rodeo, visitors enjoy entertainers, a free pancake breakfast for the first 10,000 diners, and the largest parade of horse-drawn antique carriages in the world. There is also the Western Art Show and Sale featuring more than 300 paintings, bronzes, and Navajo weavings.

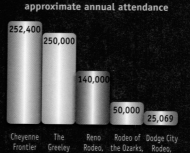

united states' largest outdoor rodeos

approximate annual attendance

Cheyenne Frontier Days, Wyoming	The Greeley Stampede, Colorado	Reno Rodeo, Nevada	Rodeo of the Ozarks, Arkansas	Dodge City Rodeo, Kansas
252,400	250,000	140,000	50,000	25,069

sports
records

basketball ● football ● bicycling
golf ● baseball ● running ● tennis
soccer ● car racing ● motorcycling
horse racing ● hockey ● x games

MINT CONDITION

Approximately 127 ounces (3,600 g) of gold worth
more than $193,250 was used to coat all the
medals for the 2012 Olympic Games. Actual solid
gold medals have not been awarded since the 1912
Games in Stockholm, Sweden. Medals are silver, and
then plated in gold.

FUELING FANS

McDonald's opened its largest restaurant ever in London just for the Olympic Games. It measured 32,290 square feet (3,000 sq m) and employed more than 2,000 people. It served about 50,000 Big Macs and 180,000 boxes of fries to athletes and spectators. It stayed open for just six weeks.

ATHLETES & AMPHIBIANS

Before constructing Olympic Park in London, officials had to relocate about 4,000 rare newts to a nearby nature preserve. Great crested newts are protected by law in Britain, and officials were not allowed to build until the newts were safe. The Olympic Park was made up of eight venues, including the Olympic Stadium, Aquatics Centre, and the Velodrome.

you're never too old to try

Hiroshi Hoketsu—an equestrian from Japan—was the oldest competitor at the Beijing Games in 2008 at age 67. He finished in 35th place in the individual dressage event. Hoketsu's Olympic dreams weren't over, though—he also qualified for the 2012 Games. He competed in his first Olympics 48 years earlier at the 1964 games in Tokyo.

HOSTING HAT TRICK

London is the only city to host the Summer Olympic Games three times. In addition to the 2012 Games, London hosted in 1908 and 1948. It is the only city in the United Kingdom to ever host the Games. In 1908, the London Games were the first to hold an opening ceremony.

STYLISH SPORTS

Famous clothing designer Stella McCartney (pictured center) created the official outfit design for Great Britain's 2012 Olympic team. The outfits, which were worn by about 900 athletes, were seen by about 750 million fans worldwide—making it one of the world's largest fashion shows.

COLORS OF COUNTRIES

Every national flag in the world includes one of the five colors of the Olympic rings, which are blue, yellow, black, green, and red. There were 205 nations taking part in the London Games.

nba team with the most championship titles

BOSTON CELTICS

The Boston Celtics are the most successful team in the NBA with 17 championship wins. The first win came in 1957, and the team went on to win the next seven consecutive titles—the longest streak of consecutive championship wins in the history of US sports. The most recent championship title came in 2008. The Celtics entered the Basketball Association of America in 1946, which later merged into the NBA in 1949. The Celtics made the NBA play-offs for four consecutive seasons from 2001 to 2005, but they were eliminated in early rounds each time.

nba teams with the most championship titles

number of championship titles

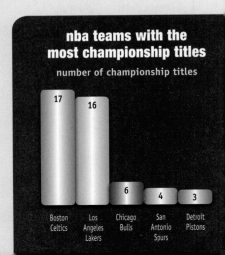

Boston Celtics	Los Angeles Lakers	Chicago Bulls	San Antonio Spurs	Detroit Pistons
17	16	6	4	3

WILT CHAMBERLAIN & MICHAEL JORDAN

Both Michael Jordan and Wilt Chamberlain averaged an amazing 30.1 points per game during their legendary careers. Jordan played for the Chicago Bulls and the Washington Wizards. He led the league in scoring for seven years. During the 1986 season, he became the second person ever to score 3,000 points in a single season. Chamberlain played for the Philadelphia Warriors, the Philadelphia 76ers, and the Los Angeles Lakers. In addition to the highest scoring average, he holds the record for the most games with 50 or more points, with 118.

nba players with the highest career scoring averages

average points per game

Wilt Chamberlain, 1959–1973	Michael Jordan, 1984–1998; 2001–2003	LeBron James, 2003–	Elgin Baylor, 1958–1971	Jerry West, 1960–1974
30.1	30.1	27.6	27.4	27.0

Michael Jordan

PORTER

BULLS 23

nba's highest-scoring game

DETROIT PISTONS

On December 13, 1983, the Detroit Pistons beat the Denver Nuggets with a score of 186–184 at McNichols Arena in Denver, Colorado. The game was tied at 145 at the end of regular play, and three overtime periods were needed to determine the winner. During the game, both the Pistons and the Nuggets each had six players who scored in the double figures. Four players scored more than 40 points each, which was an NBA first. The Pistons scored 74 field goals that night, claiming another NBA record that still stands today.

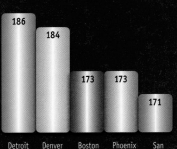

nba's highest-scoring games

points scored by a team in one game

186	184	173	173	171
Detroit Pistons, vs. Denver Nuggets, 1983	Denver Nuggets, vs. Detroit Pistons, 1983	Boston Celtics, vs. Minneapolis Lakers, 1959	Phoenix Suns, vs. Denver Nuggets, 1990	San Antonio Spurs, vs. Milwaukee Bucks, 1982

nba player with the highest salary

KOBE BRYANT

Kobe Bryant earns $25.2 million a year playing as a guard for the LA Lakers. Bryant has been a Laker since he turned pro in 1996. During his 15 years in the NBA, he has scored more than 29,440 points and grabbed more than 6,100 rebounds. Bryant has also logged almost 42,200 minutes on the court. He is a five-time NBA Champion, between 2000 and 2010, and he was the NBA Most Valuable Player during the 2007–2008 season. He has also earned All-NBA honors every year since 2002. In 2008, Bryant helped Team USA win the gold medal at the Beijing Olympics.

nba players with the highest salaries

annual salary,
in millions of US dollars

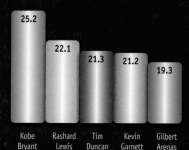

Kobe Bryant	Rashard Lewis	Tim Duncan	Kevin Garnett	Gilbert Arenas
25.2	22.1	21.3	21.2	19.3

nba player with the highest field goal percentage

artis Gilmore

Artis Gilmore leads the NBA with the highest career field goal percentage at .599. He was drafted by the Chicago Bulls in 1971, and went on to also play for the San Antonio Spurs and the Boston Celtics before retiring in 1988. A center who towers more than 7 feet (2 m) tall, Gilmore had 9,161 rebounds and 1,747 blocks. He also scored 15,579 points and had 1,777 assists. He was a five-time NBA All Star between 1978 and 1986. Gilmore, who was nicknamed the A-Train, played 909 regular season games.

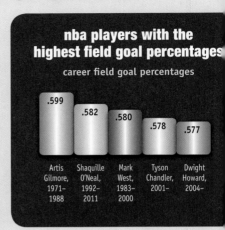

nba players with the highest field goal percentages

career field goal percentages

.599	.582	.580	.578	.577
Artis Gilmore, 1971–1988	Shaquille O'Neal, 1992–2011	Mark West, 1983–2000	Tyson Chandler, 2001–	Dwight Howard, 2004–

nba player with the most career points
kareem abdul-jabbar

During his highly successful career, Kareem Abdul-Jabbar scored a total of 38,387 points. In 1969, Abdul-Jabbar began his NBA tenure with the Milwaukee Bucks. He was named Rookie of the Year in 1970. The following year he scored 2,596 points and helped the Bucks win the NBA championship. He was traded to the Los Angeles Lakers in 1975, and with his new team, Abdul-Jabbar won the NBA championship in 1980, 1982, 1985, 1987, and 1988. He retired from basketball in 1989 and was inducted into the Basketball Hall of Fame in 1995.

nba players with the most career points
points scored

Kareem Abdul-Jabbar, 1969–1989	Karl Malone, 1985–2004	Michael Jordan, 1984–1998; 2001–2003	Wilt Chamberlain, 1959–1973	Kobe Bryant, 1996–
38,387	36,928	32,292	31,419	29,440

wnba player with the highest career ppg average

CYNTHIa COOPeR

Cynthia Cooper has the highest scoring average in the WNBA with 21 points per game. During the play-offs, she has averaged 23.3 points per game. Cooper joined the league in 1997 as a Houston Comet and remained there for four years. After a two-year hiatus, she returned for a year, and then retired in 2003. During her five years in the WNBA, she scored a total of 2,601 points. Cooper has a career high of 44 points in one game versus Sacramento in 1997. She won a gold medal in the 1988 Olympics in Seoul, the 1987 Pan American Games, and the 1990 FIBA World Championship.

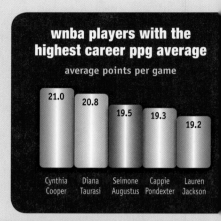

wnba players with the highest career ppg average

average points per game

Cynthia Cooper	Diana Taurasi	Seimone Augustus	Cappie Pondexter	Lauren Jackson
21.0	20.8	19.5	19.3	19.2

wnba player with the highest free throw percentage

SIDNEY SPENCER

WNBA star Sidney Spencer has the highest career free throw percentage in the league with .918. On August 17, 2007, Spencer had a career high when she sank 6 free throws in a game against Seattle. Spencer joined the WNBA in 2007 with the Los Angeles Sparks, and went on to play for the New York Liberty and the Phoenix Mercury. During her five years with the league, she has scored 714 points and grabbed 283 rebounds. In the off-season, Spencer has played for Poland and Slovakia. While in college during 2007, Spencer and her fellow Tennessee Lady Vols won the NCAA championship.

wnba players with the highest free throw percentages

career free throw percentages

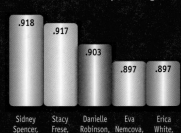

Sidney Spencer, 2007–	Stacy Frese, 2000	Danielle Robinson, 2011–	Eva Nemcova, 1997–2001	Erica White, 2008–2009
.918	.917	.903	.897	.897

wnba player with the most career points

TINA THOMPSON

A nine-time WNBA All-Star, Tina Thompson has scored 6,751 points during her 15-year career. The Los Angeles Sparks forward began her WNBA career in 1997 with the Houston Comets. She was the first draft pick in WNBA history. During her first four years with the Comets, she helped the team win the WNBA Championship each season and was the 2000 All-Star MVP. She joined the Los Angeles Sparks in 2009, and has a points-per-game average of 16.1. At the 2004 and 2008 Olympic Games, Thompson picked up gold medals for her role in helping Team USA dominate the competition.

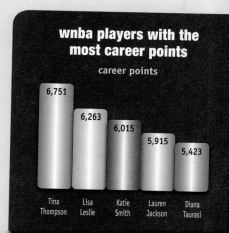

wnba players with the most career points

career points

Tina Thompson	Lisa Leslie	Katie Smith	Lauren Jackson	Diana Taurasi
6,751	6,263	6,015	5,915	5,423

UCONN WOMEN

The University of Connecticut's Huskies won 90 consecutive games between April 2008 and December 2010. After losing to Stanford in the 2008 NCAA semifinals, the UConn women's team started their next season with a win and continued their victory streak right through the national championship. The Huskies then started the 2009–2010 season ranked number one, and won every game up to their streak-ending loss to Stanford on December 19, 2010. During this streak, the team won by an average of 25 points per game. The UConn women have won a total of six NCAA championships.

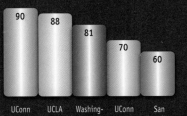

longest ncaa basketball streaks

consecutive games won

UConn women, 2008–2010	UCLA men, 1971–1974	Washington-St. Louis women, 1998–2001	UConn women, 2001–2003	San Francisco men, 1955–1957
90	88	81	70	60

women's basketball team with the most ncaa championships

TENNESSEE

The Tennessee Lady Volunteers have won eight NCAA basketball championships. The Lady Vols won their latest championship in 2008. In 1998, they had a perfect record of 39–0, which was the most seasonal wins ever in women's collegiate basketball at the time. In 2004, Tennessee was in the championship but was beaten by the University of Connecticut Huskies. Since 1976, an impressive 14 Lady Vols have been to the Olympics, and 5 Lady Vols have been inducted into the Women's Basketball Hall of Fame in Knoxville, Tennessee.

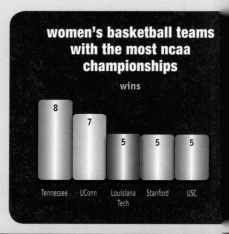

women's basketball teams with the most ncaa championships
wins

Tennessee	UConn	Louisiana Tech	Stanford	USC
8	7	5	5	5

men's basketball team with the most ncaa championships

UCLA

With 11 titles, the University of California, Los Angeles (UCLA) has the most NCAA basketball championship wins. The Bruins won their 11th championship in 1995. The school has won 23 of their last 41 league titles and has been in the NCAA play-offs for 35 of the last 41 years. During the final round of the NCAA championship in 2006, UCLA lost to the Florida Gators with a score of 73–57. Not surprisingly, UCLA has produced some basketball legends, including Kareem Abdul-Jabbar, Reggie Miller, and Baron Davis. For the last 36 years, the Bruins have called Pauley Pavilion home.

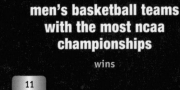

men's basketball teams with the most ncaa championships

wins

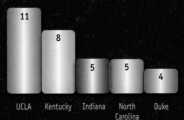

UCLA	Kentucky	Indiana	North Carolina	Duke
11	8	5	5	4

nfl player with the most passing yards

Brett Favre

Quarterback Brett Favre knows how to hit his receivers: He completed 71,838 passing yards during his amazing career. He has a completion rate of 62 percent, and has connected for 508 touchdowns. Favre is also the NFL's all-time leader in passing touchdowns (508), completions (6,300), and attempts (10,169). Favre began his career with the Atlanta Falcons in 1991. He was traded to the Green Bay Packers the next season, and played for them until 2007. Favre joined the New York Jets for the season, and was then signed by the Minnesota Vikings for the 2009 season.

nfl players with the most passing yards
yards

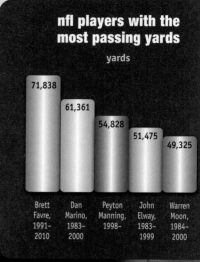

Brett Favre, 1991–2010	Dan Marino, 1983–2000	Peyton Manning, 1998–	John Elway, 1983–1999	Warren Moon, 1984–2000
71,838	61,361	54,828	51,475	49,325

nfl player with the highest career rushing total

EMMITT SMITH

Running back Emmitt Smith holds the record for all-time rushing yards with 18,355. Smith began his career with the Dallas Cowboys in 1990 and played with the team until the end of the 2002 season. In 2003, Smith signed a two-year contract with the Arizona Cardinals. Smith also holds the NFL records for the most carries with 4,142 and the most rushing touchdowns with 164. After 15 years in the NFL, Smith retired at the end of the 2004 season.

nfl players with the highest career rushing totals

rushing yards

18,355	Emmitt Smith, 1990–2004
16,726	Walter Payton, 1975–1987
15,269	Barry Sanders, 1989–1999
14,101	Curtis Martin, 1995–2007
13,684	LaDainian Tomlinson, 2001–

Jerry rice

Jerry Rice has scored a record 208 touchdowns. He is widely considered to be one of the greatest wide receivers to ever play in the National Football League. Rice holds a total of 14 NFL records, including career receptions (1,549), receiving yards (22,895), receiving touchdowns (197), consecutive 100-catch seasons (4), most games with 100 receiving yards (73), and many others. He was named NFL Player of the Year twice, *Sports Illustrated* Player of the Year four times, and NFL Offensive Player of the Year once. Rice retired from the NFL in 2005.

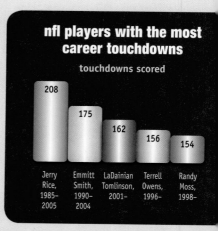

nfl players with the most career touchdowns

touchdowns scored

208	175	162	156	154
Jerry Rice, 1985– 2005	Emmitt Smith, 1990– 2004	LaDainian Tomlinson, 2001–	Terrell Owens, 1996–	Randy Moss, 1998–

nfl player with the most single-season touchdowns

LADAINIAN TOMLINSON

Running back LaDainian Tomlinson scored 31 touchdowns during the 2006 season. He was also named NFL Most Valuable Player that season for his outstanding performance. During his pro career, he has scored a total of 138 touchdowns. Tomlinson was selected fifth overall in the 2001 draft by the San Diego Chargers but was traded to the New York Jets in 2010. He holds several Chargers records, including 372 attempts (2002), 100 receptions (2003), and 1,815 rushing yards in a season (2006). Tomlinson has also been named to five Pro Bowls.

nfl players with the most single-season touchdowns

touchdowns scored

LaDainian Tomlinson, 2006	31
Shaun Alexander, 2005	28
Priest Holmes, 2003	27
Marshall Faulk, 2000	26
Emmitt Smith, 1995	25

nfl player with the highest career scoring total

MORTEN ANDERSEN

Morten Andersen led the NFL in scoring with a career total of 2,544 points. He made 565 field goals out of 709 attempts, giving him a 79.9 percent completion rate. He scored 849 extra points out of 859 attempts, resulting in a 98.8 percent success rate. Andersen, a placekicker who began his career in 1982 with the New Orleans Saints, retired in 2008 after playing for the Atlanta Falcons. Known as the Great Dane, partly because of his birthplace of Denmark, Andersen played 382 professional games. His most successful season was in 1995, when he scored 122 points.

nfl players with the highest career scoring totals
points scored

Morten Andersen, 1982–2008	Gary Anderson, 1982–2005	John Carney, 1988–2010	Jason Hanson, 1992–	Matt Stover, 1991–
2,544	2,434	2,062	2,016	2,004

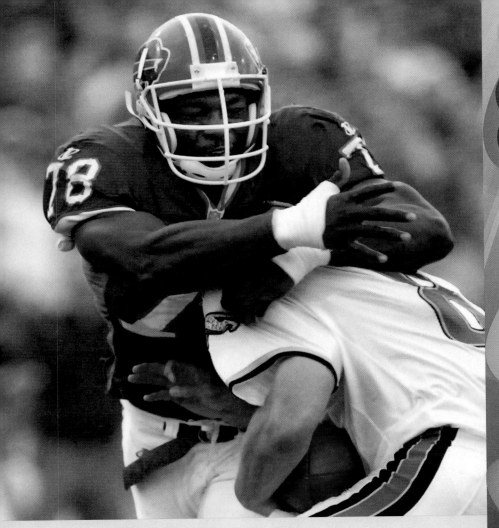

nfl player with the most quarterback sacks

BRUCE SMITH

During his 19 seasons in the NFL, defensive end Bruce Smith managed to sack the opposing quarterback 200 times. Smith was the first overall draft pick by the Buffalo Bills in 1985, and played for them until he was traded to the Washington Redskins in 2000. He was selected for the Pro Bowl 11 times and the First Team All Pro 9 times between 1987 and 1998. Smith was a four-time AFC Champion, and was named AP Defensive Player of the Year twice. He was also a part of the 1980s and 1990s All-Decade teams. Smith was inducted into the Pro Football Hall of Fame in 2009.

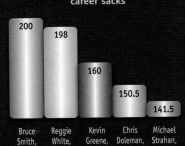

nfl players with the most quarterback sacks

career sacks

Bruce Smith, 1985–2003	Reggie White, 1985–2000	Kevin Greene, 1986–1999	Chris Doleman, 1985–1999	Michael Strahan, 1993–2007
200	198	160	150.5	141.5

nfl coach with the most wins

DON SHULa

Don Shula led his teams to a remarkable 347 wins during his 33 years as a head coach in the National Football League. When Shula became head coach of the Baltimore Colts in 1963, he became the youngest head coach in football history. He stayed with the team until 1969 and reached the play-offs four times. Shula became the head coach for the Miami Dolphins in 1970 and coached them until 1995. During this time, the Dolphins reached the play-offs 20 times and won at least 10 games a season 21 times. After leading them to Super Bowl wins in 1972 and 1973, Shula became one of only five coaches to win the championship in back-to-back years.

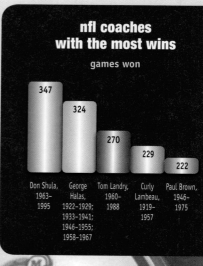

nfl coaches with the most wins
games won

Don Shula, 1963–1995	George Halas, 1922–1929; 1933–1941; 1946–1955; 1958–1967	Tom Landry, 1960–1988	Curly Lambeau, 1919–1957	Paul Brown, 1946–1975
347	324	270	229	222

nfl player with the highest salary

PEYTON MANNING

Peyton Manning's salary of $23 million tops all other players in the NFL. Manning turned pro in 1998 and was signed by the Indianapolis Colts. In 2012, he joined the Denver Broncos. He has a career average rating of 94.9 and achieved his highest rating of 121.1 in 2004. Manning holds the team records for career passing yards, career wins, pass completions, and passing touchdowns. He also holds the NFL record for the most MVP Awards, with four, which he received between 2003 and 2009. Manning has been selected to the Pro Bowl 11 times, and won the Super Bowl in 2006 against the Chicago Bears.

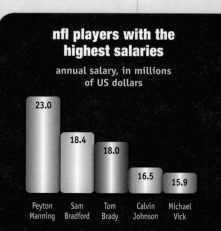

nfl players with the highest salaries

annual salary, in millions of US dollars

Peyton Manning	Sam Bradford	Tom Brady	Calvin Johnson	Michael Vick
23.0	18.4	18.0	16.5	15.9

nfl team with the most consecutive wins

New England Patriots

Between 2006 and 2007, the New England Patriots won 19 consecutive games. They ended the 2006 regular season with three wins. During the 2007 regular season, the team won all 16 games—only the fifth team in league history to do so. During this impressive season, the team set an NFL record by scoring 589 points and 75 touchdowns. The Patriots have a winning history, including 10 AFC East championships, 15 NFL play-off appearances, and 3 Super Bowl wins.

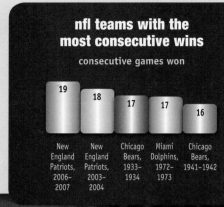

nfl teams with the most consecutive wins

consecutive games won

19	18	17	17	16
New England Patriots, 2006–2007	New England Patriots, 2003–2004	Chicago Bears, 1933–1934	Miami Dolphins, 1972–1973	Chicago Bears, 1941–1942

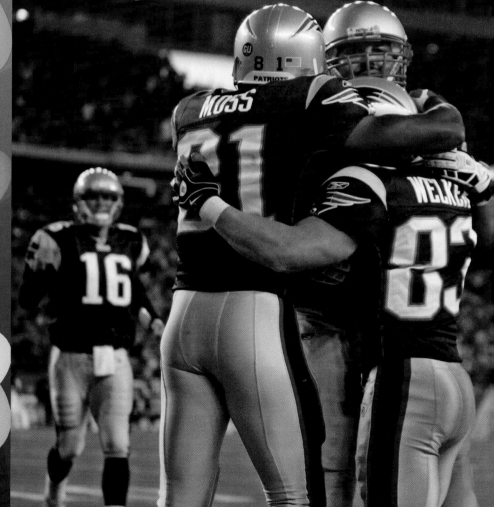

nfl team with the most super bowl wins

PITTSBURGH STEELERS

With six championship wins between 1974 and 2009, the Pittsburgh Steelers have won more Super Bowls than any other team in NFL history. The Steelers have also played and won more AFC championship games than any other team in the conference. The Steelers were founded in 1933 and are the fifth-oldest franchise in the league. Twenty-three retired Steelers have been inducted into the Pro Football Hall of Fame, including Franco Harris, Chuck Noll, and Terry Bradshaw.

nfl teams with the most super bowl wins

super bowls won

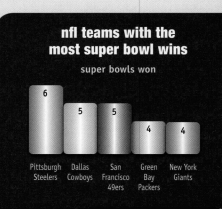

Pittsburgh Steelers	Dallas Cowboys	San Francisco 49ers	Green Bay Packers	New York Giants
6	5	5	4	4

cyclist with the most tour de france wins

Lance Armstrong

Lance Armstrong was the first cyclist ever to win seven Tour de France races. He won his first race in 1999, just three years after being diagnosed with cancer. He went on to win the top cycling event for the next six years, retiring after his 2005 victory. Armstrong has received many awards and honors during his career, including being named *Sports Illustrated*'s Sportsman of the Year in 2002. Armstrong also formed the Lance Armstrong Foundation, which supports people recovering from cancer.

cyclists with the most tour de france wins

number of wins

Lance Armstrong, USA	Eddy Merckx, Belgium	Jacques Anquetil, France	Bernard Hinault, France	Miguel Indurain, Spain
7	5	5	5	5

LUKE DONALD

During 2011, golfer Luke Donald had the lowest seasonal average in the PGA with a score of 68.86. Donald, who was born in England, had a huge year in 2011. He was named PGA Player of the Year, European Tour Golfer of the Year, and he took home the Vardon Trophy. During 2011, Donald was also the leading money winner with $6.68 million. Donald joined the PGA Tour in 2001, and the European Tour in 2003. On the PGA Tour, he's had 5 tournament wins, and on the European Tour, he's had 6. During his career, he's played in 38 tournaments and finished in the top 25 a total of 12 times.

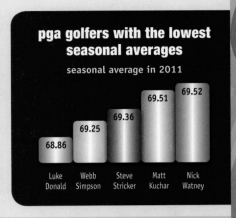

pga golfers with the lowest seasonal averages

seasonal average in 2011

Luke Donald	Webb Simpson	Steve Stricker	Matt Kuchar	Nick Watney
68.86	69.25	69.36	69.51	69.52

lpga golfer with the lowest seasonal average

YANI TSENG

With a 69.66, Yani Tseng had the lowest seasonal average in the LPGA in 2011 and picked up her first Vare Trophy for that accomplishment. During that year, she also became the youngest player to win consecutive Rolex Player of the Year awards. And, Tseng won seven LPGA events, and led the money winners list with $2.92 million. She joined the LPGA in 2001, and has won 15 tournaments during her career. She's finished in the top ten a total of 54 times. Tseng's career earnings total more than $8.5 million.

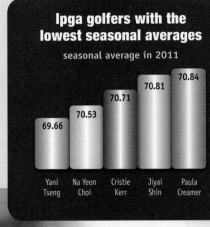

lpga golfers with the lowest seasonal averages

seasonal average in 2011

Yani Tseng	Na Yeon Choi	Cristie Kerr	Jiyai Shin	Paula Creamer
69.66	70.53	70.71	70.81	70.84

lpga's highest-paid golfer

annika sorenstam

Annika Sorenstam has earned $22.5 million since her LPGA career began in 1994. During this time, she has had 72 career victories, including nine majors. In 2005, Sorenstam earned her eighth Rolex Player of the Year award—the most in LPGA history. She also became the first player to sweep Rolex Player of the Year honors, the Vare Trophy, and the ADT Official Money List title five times. Sorenstam earned her fifth consecutive Mizuno Classic title, making her the first golfer in LPGA history to win the same event five consecutive years. Sorenstam retired at the end of the 2008 season.

lpga's highest-paid golfers
career earnings, in millions of US dollars

Annika Sorenstam	Karrie Webb	Lorena Ochoa	Cristie Kerr	Juli Inkster
22.5	16.6	14.8	13.6	13.3

golfer with the most major tournament wins

JACK NICKLAUS

Golfing great Jack Nicklaus has won a total of 18 major championships. His wins include six Masters, five PGAs, four US Opens, and three British Opens. Nicklaus was named PGA Player of the Year five times. He was a member of the winning US Ryder Cup team six times and was an individual World Cup winner a record three times. He was inducted into the World Golf Hall of Fame in 1974, just 12 years after he turned professional. He joined the US Senior PGA Tour in 1990. In addition to playing the game, Nicklaus has designed close to 200 golf courses and has written a number of popular books about the sport.

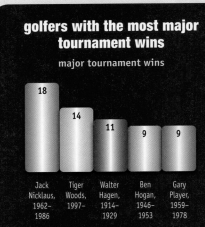

golfers with the most major tournament wins

major tournament wins

18	14	11	9	9
Jack Nicklaus, 1962–1986	Tiger Woods, 1997–	Walter Hagen, 1914–1929	Ben Hogan, 1946–1953	Gary Player, 1959–1978

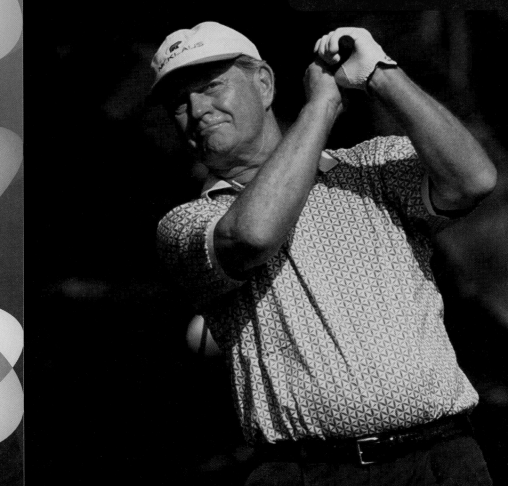

mlb player with the highest seasonal home-run total

Barry Bonds

On October 5, 2001, Barry Bonds smashed Mark McGwire's record for seasonal home runs when he hit his 71st home run in the first inning of a game against the Los Angeles Dodgers. In the third inning, he hit number 72, and two days later he reached 73. Bonds, a left fielder for the San Francisco Giants, has a career total of 762 home runs. He also holds the records for seasonal walks (232) and seasonal on-base percentage (.609). Bonds and his father, hitting coach Bobby Bonds, hold the all-time father-son home-run record with 1,020.

mlb players with the highest seasonal home-run totals

number of home runs

Barry Bonds, 2001	Mark McGwire, 1998	Sammy Sosa, 1998	Mark McGwire, 1999	Sammy Sosa, 2001
73	70	66	65	64

mlb team with the highest payroll

NEW YORK YANKEES

The combined 2012 payroll of the New York Yankees totals more than $197 million. Some of the highest-paid players include Alex Rodriguez ($30 million), C. C. Sabathia ($23 million), and Mark Teixeira ($23.1 million). The Yankees have been very successful with their pricey roster, winning 40 American League pennants and 27 World Series. The team also has a new place to showcase its talent—a new Yankee Stadium opened in 2009. The stadium cost $1.5 billion, making it the second-most expensive stadium in the world.

mlb teams with the highest payrolls

payroll in 2012, in millions of US dollars

New York Yankees	Philadelphia Phillies	Boston Red Sox	Los Angeles Angels	Detroit Tigers
197.9	174.5	173.1	154.4	132.3

mlb player with the most home runs

BARRY BONDS

Barry Bonds has hit more home runs than anyone who ever played in the MLB, cracking 762 balls over the wall during his ongoing career. Bonds has hit more than 30 home runs in a season 13 times—another MLB record. During his impressive career, Bonds has won 8 Gold Gloves, 12 Silver Slugger awards, and 13 All-Star awards. Bonds began his career with the Pittsburgh Pirates in 1986; he was transferred to the San Francisco Giants in 1993 and has played for the team since then. He is only one of three players to join the 700 Home Run Club.

mlb players with the most home runs

number of home runs*

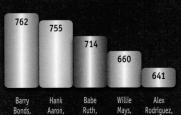

Barry Bonds, 1986–2007	Hank Aaron, 1954–1976	Babe Ruth, 1914–1935	Willie Mays, 1948–1973	Alex Rodriguez, 1994–
762	755	714	660	641

*As of June 24, 2012

mlb pitcher with the most career strikeouts

NOLAN RYAN

Nolan Ryan leads Major League Baseball with an incredible 5,714 career strikeouts. In his impressive 28-year career, he played for the New York Mets, the California Angels, the Houston Astros, and the Texas Rangers. The right-handed pitcher from Refugio, Texas, led the American League in strikeouts ten times. In 1989, at the age of 42, Ryan became the oldest pitcher ever to lead the Major Leagues in strikeouts. Ryan set another record in 1991 when he pitched his seventh career no-hitter.

mlb pitchers with the most career strikeouts

number of strikeouts

Nolan Ryan, 1966–1993	Randy Johnson, 1989–2009	Roger Clemens, 1984–2007	Steve Carlton, 1965–1988	Bert Blyleven, 1970–1992
5,714	4,875	4,672	4,136	3,701

mlb player with the most career hits

PETE ROSE

Pete Rose belted an amazing 4,256 hits during his 23 years of professional baseball. He made his record-setting hit in 1985, when he was a player-manager for the Cincinnati Reds. By the time Rose retired as a player from Major League Baseball in 1986, he had set several other career records. Rose holds the Major League records for the most career games (3,562), the most times at bat (14,053), and the most seasons with more than 200 hits (10). During his career, he played for the Cincinnati Reds, the Philadelphia Phillies, and the Montreal Expos.

mlb players with the most career hits

number of hits

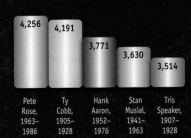

Pete Rose, 1963–1986	Ty Cobb, 1905–1928	Hank Aaron, 1952–1976	Stan Musial, 1941–1963	Tris Speaker, 1907–1928
4,256	4,191	3,771	3,630	3,514

mlb player with the highest batting average

TY COBB

Baseball legend Ty Cobb had a batting average of .367 during his 23-year career, and it has remained the highest average in MLB history for more than 80 years. Known as the "Georgia Peach," the American League outfielder set 90 different MLB records during his outstanding career. He won 12 national batting titles, including 9 consecutive wins between 1907 and 1915. Cobb began his career with the Detroit Tigers in 1905, and later moved to the Philadelphia Athletics in 1927. Cobb was voted into the Baseball Hall of Fame in 1936 with 98.2 percent of the votes.

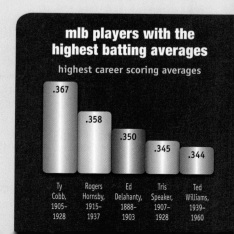

mlb players with the highest batting averages

highest career scoring averages

Ty Cobb, 1905–1928	Rogers Hornsby, 1915–1937	Ed Delahanty, 1888–1903	Tris Speaker, 1907–1928	Ted Williams, 1939–1960
.367	.358	.350	.345	.344

mlb player with the most career runs

RICKEY HENDERSON

During his 25 years in the majors, baseball great Rickey Henderson boasts the most career runs with 2,295. Henderson got his start with the Oakland Athletics in 1979, and went on to play for the Yankees, the Mets, the Mariners, the Red Sox, the Padres, the Dodgers, and the Angels. Henderson won a Gold Glove award in 1981, and the American League MVP award in 1989 and 1990. Henderson is also known as the "Man of Steal" because he holds the MLB record for most stolen bases in a career, with 1,406.

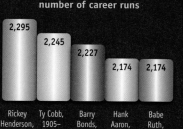

mlb players with the most career runs

number of career runs

Rickey Henderson, 1979–2003	Ty Cobb, 1905–1928	Barry Bonds, 1986–2007	Hank Aaron, 1954–1976	Babe Ruth, 1914–1935
2,295	2,245	2,227	2,174	2,174

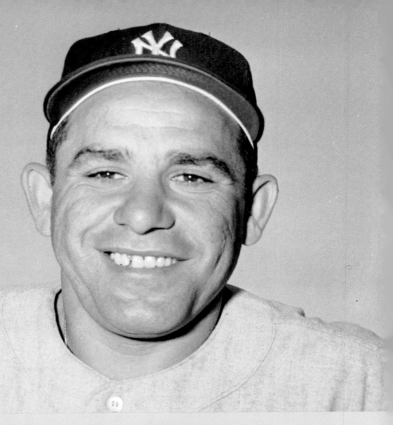

Yogi Berra

most mvp awards in the american league

YOGI BERRA, JOE DIMAGGIO, JIMMIE FOXX, MICKEY MANTLE & ALEX RODRIGUEZ

With three honors each, Yogi Berra, Joe DiMaggio, Jimmie Foxx, Mickey Mantle, and Alex Rodriguez all hold the record for the Most Valuable Player awards during their professional careers. Berra, DiMaggio, Mantle, and Rodriguez were all New York Yankees. Foxx played for the Athletics, the Cubs, and the Phillies. The player with the biggest gap between wins was DiMaggio, who won his first award in 1939 and his last in 1947. Also nicknamed "Joltin' Joe" and the "Yankee Clipper," DiMaggio began playing in the Major Leagues in 1936. The following year, he led the league in home runs and runs scored. He was inducted into the Baseball Hall of Fame in 1955.

mlb players with the most american league mvp awards

number of mvp awards

3	3	3	3	3
Yogi Berra, 1946–1963; 1965	Joe DiMaggio, 1936–1951	Jimmie Foxx, 1925–1945	Mickey Mantle, 1951–1968	Alex Rodriguez, 1994–

BarrY BONDS

San Francisco Giant Barry Bonds has earned seven Most Valuable Player awards for his amazing achievements in the National League. He received his first two MVP awards in 1990 and 1992 while playing for the Pittsburgh Pirates. The next five awards came while wearing the Giants uniform in 1993, 2001, 2002, 2003, and 2004. Bonds is the first player to win an MVP award three times in consecutive seasons. In fact, Bonds is the only baseball player in history to have won more than three MVP awards.

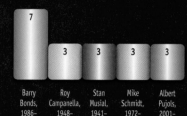

mlb players with the most national league mvp awards

number of mvp awards

Barry Bonds, 1986–2007	Roy Campanella, 1948–1957	Stan Musial, 1941–1963	Mike Schmidt, 1972–1989	Albert Pujols, 2001–
7	3	3	3	3

mlb team with the most world series wins

New York Yankees

Between 1923 and 2010, the New York Yankees were the World Series champions a record 27 times. The team picked up their latest win in October of 2009 when they beat the Philadelphia Phillies. The Yankees beat the Phillies four games to two to get their first win in nine years. Since their early days, the team has included some of baseball's greatest players, including Babe Ruth, Lou Gehrig, Yogi Berra, Joe DiMaggio, and Mickey Mantle.

mlb teams with the most world series wins
number of wins

NY Yankees	St. Louis Cardinals	Philadelphia/ Kansas City/ Oakland Athletics	Boston Red Sox	Brooklyn/ LA Dodgers
27	11	9	7	6

mlb pitcher with the most cy young awards

roger clemens

Roger Clemens, a starting pitcher for the Houston Astros, has earned a record seven Cy Young Awards during his career so far. He set a Major League record in April 1986 when he struck out 20 batters in one game. He later tied this record in September 1996. In September 2001, Clemens became the first Major League pitcher to win 20 of his first 21 decisions in one season. In June 2003, he became the first pitcher in more than a decade to win his 300th game. He also struck out his 4,000th batter that year.

mlb pitchers with the most cy young awards

number of cy young awards

Roger Clemens, 1984–2007	Randy Johnson, 1988–2010	Steve Carlton, 1965–1988	Greg Maddux, 1986–2008	Pedro Martinez, 1992–2011
7	5	4	4	3

mlb player with the most at bats

pete rose

Pete Rose has stood behind the plate for 14,053 at bats—more than any other Major League player. Rose signed with the Cincinnati Reds after graduating from high school in 1963, and played second base. During his impressive career, Rose set several other records, including the most singles in the Major Leagues (3,315), most seasons with 600 or more at bats in the Major Leagues (17), most career doubles in the National League (746), and most career runs in the National League (2,165). He was also named World Series MVP, *Sports Illustrated*'s Sportsman of the Year, and the *Sporting News* Man of the Year.

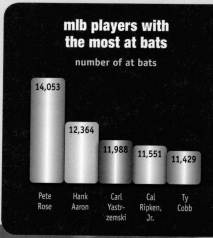

mlb players with the most at bats

number of at bats

14,053	12,364	11,988	11,551	11,429
Pete Rose	Hank Aaron	Carl Yastr- zemski	Cal Ripken, Jr.	Ty Cobb

mlb player with the most career RBIs

HANK AARON

During his 23 years in the Major Leagues, right-handed Hank Aaron batted in an incredible 2,297 runs. Aaron began his professional career with the Indianapolis Clowns, a team in the Negro American League, in 1952. He was traded to the Milwaukee Braves in 1954 and won the National League batting championship with an average of .328. He was named the league's Most Valuable Player a year later when he led his team to a World Series victory. Aaron retired as a player in 1976 and was inducted into the Baseball Hall of Fame in 1982.

mlb players with the most career RBIs

number of runs batted in

2,297	2,213	2,076	1,996	1,995
Hank Aaron, 1952–1976	Babe Ruth, 1914–1935	Cap Anson, 1876–1897	Barry Bonds, 1986–2007	Lou Gehrig, 1923–1939

mlb player with the most consecutive games played

CaL rIPKen, Jr.

Baltimore Oriole Cal Ripken, Jr., played 2,632 consecutive games from May 30, 1982, to September 20, 1998. The right-handed third baseman also holds the record for the most consecutive innings played: 8,243. In June 1996, Ripken broke the world record for consecutive games with 2,216, surpassing Sachio Kinugasa of Japan. When he played as a shortstop, Ripken set Major League records for most home runs (345) and most extra base hits (855) for his position. He started in the All-Star Game a record 19 times in a row.

mlb players with the most consecutive games played

number of consecutive games played

Cal Ripken, Jr., 1978–2001	Lou Gehrig, 1923–1939	Everett Scott, 1914–1925	Steve Garvey, 1968–1988	Miguel Tejada, 1997–
2,632	2,130	1,307	1,207	1,152

runner with the fastest mile

HICHAM EL GUERROUJ

Moroccan runner Hicham El Guerrouj is super-speedy—he ran a mile in just over 3 minutes and 43 seconds in July 1999 while racing in Rome. He also holds the record for the fastest mile in North America with a time just short of 3 minutes and 50 seconds. El Guerrouj is an Olympian with gold medals in the 1,500-meter and 5,000-meter races. With this accomplishment at the 2004 Athens games, he became the first runner to win both races at the same Olympics in more than 75 years. El Guerrouj returned to the Olympics in 2006 as a torchbearer in Torino, Italy.

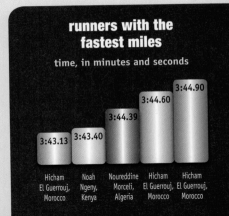

runners with the fastest miles

time, in minutes and seconds

Hicham El Guerrouj, Morocco	Noah Ngeny, Kenya	Noureddine Morceli, Algeria	Hicham El Guerrouj, Morocco	Hicham El Guerrouj, Morocco
3:43.13	3:43.40	3:44.39	3:44.60	3:44.90

top-earning female tennis player

serena williams

Serena Williams has earned $35 million since she began playing professional tennis in 1995. During her amazing career, Williams has won 40 singles championships and 20 doubles championships, as well as two gold medals in the 2000 and 2008 Olympics. She has also won all four of the Grand Slam championships. Williams has won many impressive awards, including AP's Female Athlete of the Year, the BBC's Sports Personality of the Year, and two Espy Awards.

top-earning female tennis players

career earnings, in millions of US dollars

35.0	27.9	24.2	22.1	21.8
Serena Williams, 1995–	Venus Williams, 1994–	Kim Clijsters 1997–	Lindsay Davenport, 1993–	Steffi Graf, 1982–1999

top-earning male tennis player

roger feDerer

Tennis great Roger Federer has earned $69.7 million since his career began in 1998. He has won 73 singles titles and 8 doubles titles, including 17 Grand Slams. His major victories include four Australian Opens, one French Open, six Wimbledon titles, and five US Opens. From February 2, 2004, to August 17, 2008, Federer was ranked first in the world for 237 consecutive weeks. He is also the only player in history to win five consecutive titles at two different Grand Slam tournaments (Wimbledon and US Open).

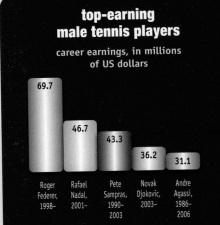

top-earning male tennis players

career earnings, in millions of US dollars

Roger Federer, 1998–	69.7
Rafael Nadal, 2001–	46.7
Pete Sampras, 1990–2003	43.3
Novak Djokovic, 2003–	36.2
Andre Agassi, 1986–2006	31.1

woman with the most grand slam singles titles

MARGARET COURT SMITH

Margaret Court Smith won 24 Grand Slam singles titles between 1960 and 1975. She is the only woman ever to win the French, British, US, and Australian titles during one year in both the singles and doubles competitions. She was only the second woman to win all four singles titles in the same year. During her amazing career, she won a total of 66 Grand Slam championships—more than any other woman. Court was the world's top-seeded female player from 1962 to 1965, 1969 to 1970, and 1973. She was inducted into the International Tennis Hall of Fame in 1979.

women with the most grand slam singles titles

number of titles won

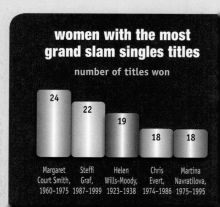

Margaret Court Smith, 1960–1975	Steffi Graf, 1987–1999	Helen Wills-Moody, 1923–1938	Chris Evert, 1974–1986	Martina Navratilova, 1975–1995
24	22	19	18	18

man with the most grand slam singles titles

Roger Federer

Swiss tennis great Roger Federer has won a record 17 Grand Slam championship titles and earned more than $69.7 million since he turned pro in 1998. He has four Australian Open wins, one French Open win, seven Wimbledon wins, and five US Open wins. Federer is also one of only two players to win the Golden Slam—winning all four Grand Slam championships and an Olympic gold medal in the same year (2008). Federer achieved his 17th Grand Slam title when he defeated Andy Murray at the Wimbledon gentleman's final in 2012.

men with the most grand slam singles titles

number of titles won

Roger Federer, 2003–	Pete Sampras, 1990–2002	Roy Emerson, 1961–1967	Björn Borg, 1974–1981	Rafael Nadal 2001–
17	14	12	12	11

DaVID BeCKHaM

Soccer superstar David Beckham earned $46 million during 2011. The LA Galaxy paid him $9 million, and another $37 million came from endorsements. Beckham has a multi-year deal with clothing retailer H&M, and earns royalties from Adidas for the soccer clothes and cleats named after him. He also served as Samsung's global ambassador for the 2012 Olympic Games. Beckham began his career with England's Manchester United in 1992, then played briefly for Spain's Real Madrid, and joined the Galaxy in 2007. He won his first MLS cup in November 2011 with the team. After this victory, Beckham became one of the few players in soccer history to win three league titles in three different countries.

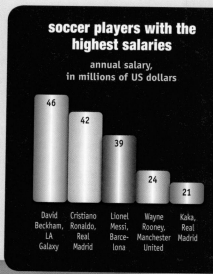

soccer players with the highest salaries

annual salary,
in millions of US dollars

David Beckham, LA Galaxy	Cristiano Ronaldo, Real Madrid	Lionel Messi, Barcelona	Wayne Rooney, Manchester United	Kaka, Real Madrid
46	42	39	24	21

woman with the most CAPS

KrISTINE LILLY

With a total of 352, Kristine Lilly holds the world record for the most international games played, or CAPS. This is the highest number of CAPS in both the men's and women's international soccer organizations. She has a career total of 130 international goals—the second highest in the world. In 2004, Lilly scored her 100th international goal, becoming one of only five women to ever accomplish that feat. In 2005, Lilly was named US Soccer's Female Athlete of the Year. She retired in January 2011.

women with the most CAPS

number of career CAPS

Kristine Lilly, USA, 1987– 2011	Mia Hamm, USA, 1987– 2004	Julie Foudy, USA, 1988– 2004	Christie Rampone, USA, 1997–	Joy Fawcett, USA, 1987– 2004
352	275	272	243	239

man with the most CAPS

AHMED HASSAN

Ahmed Hassan, the captain for the Egyptian National soccer team and a midfielder for the Egyptian Premier League's Zamalek SC, has the most CAPS—or international games—with 181 appearances. He made his international debut in 1995. Hassan helped the National team win four CAF Africa Cup of Nations between 1998 and 2010, and was named the tournament's best player twice. He has also played in the Belgium Cup, the Turkish Cup, and the CAF Championship League. In 2010, Hassan was voted Best African-Based Player of the Year.

men with the most CAPS

number of career CAPS

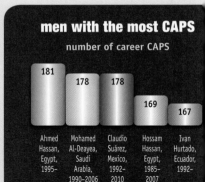

Ahmed Hassan, Egypt, 1995–	Mohamed Al-Deayea, Saudi Arabia, 1990–2006	Claudio Suárez, Mexico, 1992–2010	Hossam Hassan, Egypt, 1985–2007	Ivan Hurtado, Ecuador, 1992–
181	178	178	169	167

GERMANY

Germany has accumulated a total of 33 points during World Cup soccer competition. A win is worth 4 points, runner-up is worth 3 points, third place is worth 2 points, and fourth place is worth 1 point. Germany won the World Cup four times between 1954 and 1990. Most recently, Germany earned 2 points for a third-place finish in 2010. The World Cup is organized by the Fédération Internationale de Football Association (FIFA) and is played every four years.

countries with the most world cup points

total number of points

Germany/ W. Germany, 1954–2006	Brazil, 1958–2002	Italy, 1934–2006	Argentina, 1978–1986	Uruguay, 1930–1950
33	30	25	14	10

driver with the most formula one wins

MICHAEL SCHUMACHER

Race-car driver Michael Schumacher won 91 Formula One races in his professional career, which began in 1991. Out of the 250 races he competed in, he reached the podium 154 times. In 2002, Schumacher became the only Formula One driver to have a podium finish in each race in which he competed that season. He won seven world championships between 1994 and 2004. Schumacher, who was born in Germany, began his career with Benetton but later switched to Ferrari. He retired from racing in 2006.

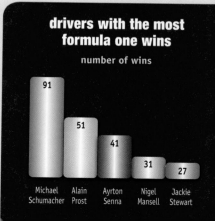

drivers with the most formula one wins
number of wins

Michael Schumacher	Alain Prost	Ayrton Senna	Nigel Mansell	Jackie Stewart
91	51	41	31	27

BUDDY BAKER

Race-car legend Buddy Baker dominated the competition at the 1980 Daytona 500 with an average speed of over 177 miles (285 km) per hour. It was the first Daytona 500 race run under three hours. Baker had a history of speed before this race—he became the first driver to race more than 200 miles (322 km) per hour on a closed course in 1970. During his amazing career, Baker competed in 688 Winston Cup races—he won 19 of them and finished in the top five in 198 others. He also won more than $3.6 million. He was inducted into the International Motorsports Hall of Fame in 1997.

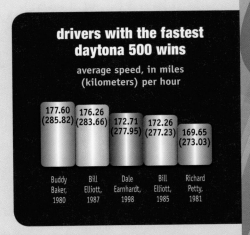

drivers with the fastest daytona 500 wins

average speed, in miles (kilometers) per hour

177.60 (285.82)	176.26 (283.66)	172.71 (277.95)	172.26 (277.23)	169.65 (273.03)
Buddy Baker, 1980	Bill Elliott, 1987	Dale Earnhardt, 1998	Bill Elliott, 1985	Richard Petty, 1981

driver with the most consecutive sprint cup championships

JIMMIE JOHNSON

Jimmie Johnson has won five consecutive Sprint Cup Championships between 2006 and 2010. With his 54 series wins, he is ranked 10th in career victories. During his career, Johnson has also had 138 top-five finishes and 208 top-ten finishes. He has been named Driver of the Year four times, which is a record he holds with teammate Jeff Gordon. Johnson joined the Hendrick Motorsports team in 2002, and drives a Chevrolet owned by Gordon. In addition to his Sprint Cup victories, Johnson has won the Daytona 500 one time and the Coca-Cola 500 and the All State 400 three times each.

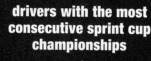

drivers with the most consecutive sprint cup championships

consecutive wins

5	3	2	2	2
Jimmie Johnson, 2006–2010	Cale Yarborough, 1976–1978	Jeff Gordon, 1997–1998	Dale Earnhardt 1993–1994	Darrell Waltrip 1981–1982

Jimmie Johnson

WINNER
June 28, 2009

T2 Technology

youngest driver to win a sprint cup race

JOEY LOGANO

A little over a month after his 19th birthday, Joey Logano became the youngest winner of a Sprint Cup race. He accomplished this on June 28, 2009, in New Hampshire. Later that year, he also became the youngest recipient of the Raybestos Rookie of the Year Award. In 2010, Logano became the youngest pole winner in Sprint Cup history at Bristol Motor Speedway. He drives a Toyota for the Joe Gibbs Racing Team, which is sponsored by The Home Depot. Logano began his NASCAR career in 2007, and won seven races on six different tracks that year.

youngest drivers to win a sprint cup race
age at time of win

Joey Logano, 2009	Trevor Bayne, 2011	Kyle Busch, 2005	Donald Thomas, 1952	Fireball Roberts, 1950
19 years, 35 days	20 years, 1 day	20 years, 125 days	20 years, 129 days	21 years, 205 days

highest paid NASCAR driver

DALE EARNHARDT, JR.

In 2011, NASCAR driver Dale Earnhardt, Jr. won $28 million. This total includes race winnings, as well as income earned for several endorsements including Wrangler, Chevrolet, and Dollar General. During his career, he has won more than $100 million. Gordon drives the number 88 Chevy Impala for Hendrick Motors in the NASCAR Sprint Cup Series. He's competed in more than 450 NASCAR Sprint Cup races and 120 NASCAR Nationwide Series races during his 16-year career. Earnhardt, Jr. has 19 career wins, and 101 top-five finishes. He won the Daytona 500 in 2004, and the Busch Series Championship in 1998 and 1999.

highest paid NASCAR drivers

salary in 2011, in millions of US dollars

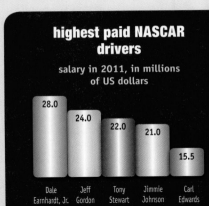

Dale Earnhardt, Jr.	Jeff Gordon	Tony Stewart	Jimmie Johnson	Carl Edwards
28.0	24.0	22.0	21.0	15.5

rider with the most superbike race points

Carlos Checa

Spanish superbike rider Carlos Checa had the most race points in 2011 with 505, and was the winner of the Superbike World Championship. During the 2011 race season, he competed for the Althea Team on a Ducati 1098R. Out of his 26 races that year, he won 15 of them, and reached the podium 21 times. Checa began racing 125cc and 250cc bikes for Honda in 1993, and moved to superbike racing in 2008. Checa has raced for Honda, Yamaha, and Ducati. During his superbike career, Checa has accumulated 1,399 points and won 23 races.

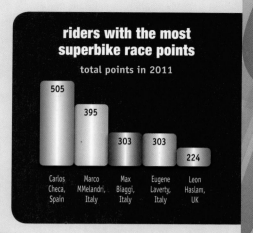

riders with the most superbike race points

total points in 2011

Carlos Checa, Spain	Marco MMelandri, Italy	Max Biaggi, Italy	Eugene Laverty, Italy	Leon Haslam, UK
505	395	303	303	224

rider with the most motocross world titles

STEFAN EVERTS

Stefan Everts is the king of motocross with a total of ten world titles. He won twice on a 500cc bike, seven more times on a 250cc bike, and once on a 125cc bike. During his 18-year career, he had 101 Grand Prix victories. Everts was named Belgium Sportsman of the Year five times. He retired after his final world title in 2006 and is now a consultant and coach for the riders who compete for the KTM racing team.

riders with the most motocross world titles

number of wins

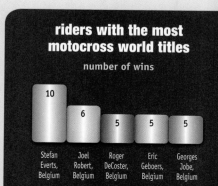

Stefan Everts, Belgium	Joel Robert, Belgium	Roger DeCoster, Belgium	Eric Geboers, Belgium	Georges Jobe, Belgium
10	6	5	5	5

EDDIE arcaro

Between 1938 and 1961, jockey Eddie Arcaro won a total of 17 Triple Crown races. Nicknamed "the Master," Arcaro won the Kentucky Derby five times, the Preakness six times, and the Belmont six times. He holds the record for the most Preakness wins, and is tied for the most Kentucky Derby and Belmont wins. He was also horse racing's top money winner six times between 1940 and 1955. During his career, Arcaro competed in 24,092 races and won 4,779 of them.

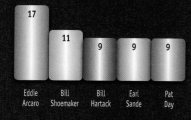

jockeys with the most triple crown wins
number of wins

Eddie Arcaro	Bill Shoemaker	Bill Hartack	Earl Sande	Pat Day
17	11	9	9	9

nhl team with the most stanley cup wins

MONTREAL CANADIENS

The Montreal Canadiens won an amazing 24 Stanley Cup victories between 1916 and 1993. That's almost one-quarter of all the Stanley Cup championships ever played. The team plays at Montreal's Molson Centre. The Canadiens were created in December 1909 by J. Ambrose O'Brien to play for the National Hockey Association (NHA). They eventually made the transition into the National Hockey League. Over the years, the Canadiens have included such great players as Maurice Richard, George Hainsworth, Jacques Lemaire, Saku Koivu, and Emile Bouchard.

nhl teams with the most stanley cup wins

number of Stanley Cup wins

Montreal Canadiens	Toronto Maple Leafs	Detroit Red Wings	Boston Bruins	Edmonton Oilers
24	13	11	6	5

nhl player with the most career points

WAYNE GRETZKY

Wayne Gretzky scored an unbelievable 2,857 points and 894 goals during his 20-year career. Gretzky was the first person in the NHL to average more than two points per game. Many people consider Canadian-born Gretzky to be the greatest player in the history of the National Hockey League. In fact, he is called "the Great One." He officially retired from the sport in 1999 and was inducted into the Hockey Hall of Fame that same year. After his final game, the NHL retired his jersey number (99). In 2005, Gretzky became the head coach of the Phoenix Coyotes.

nhl players with the most career points

number of points scored

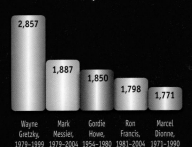

Wayne Gretzky, 1979–1999	Mark Messier, 1979–2004	Gordie Howe, 1954–1980	Ron Francis, 1981–2004	Marcel Dionne, 1971–1990
2,857	1,887	1,850	1,798	1,771

nhl goalie with the most career wins

MARTIN BRODEUR

Not much gets by goalie Martin Brodeur—he's won 656 games since he was drafted by the New Jersey Devils in 1990. Still playing with the Devils, Brodeur has helped the team win three Stanley Cup championships. He is also the only goalie in NHL history to complete seven seasons with 40 or more wins. Brodeur has been an NHL All-Star ten times. He has received the Vezina Trophy four times and the Jennings Trophy five times. He also ranks second in the league in regular-season shutouts.

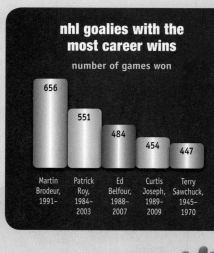

nhl goalies with the most career wins

number of games won

Martin Brodeur, 1991–	Patrick Roy, 1984–2003	Ed Belfour, 1988–2007	Curtis Joseph, 1989–2009	Terry Sawchuck, 1945–1970
656	551	484	454	447

nhl player with the most power play goals

DAVE ANDREYCHUK

Dave Andreychuk has scored more power play goals than any other player in the NHL history with 274. A power play occurs when one team has all five players on the ice, and the other team has at least one player in the penalty box. The full-strength team has a huge advantage to score with the extra player on the ice. Andreychuk was in the NHL from 1982 to 2006, and played for the Buffalo Sabres, the Toronto Maple Leafs, the New Jersey Devils, the Boston Bruins, the Colorado Avalanche, and the Tampa Bay Lightning. With a total of 1,435 points, he is one of the highest-scoring left wings in NHL history.

nhl players with the most power play goals

power play goals

Player	Power play goals
Dave Andreychuk, 1982–2006	274
Brett Hull, 1985–2006	265
Teemu Selanne, 1988–1992	248
Luc Robitaille, 1986–2006	247
Brendan Shanahan, 1987–2009	237

skateboarder with the most x game gold medals

TONY HaWK

American Tony Hawk won ten gold medals for skateboarding in the Extreme Games between 1995 and 2002. All his medals came in vertical competition, meaning that the riders compete on a vert ramp similar to a half-pipe. Hawk is most famous for nailing the 900—completing 2.5 rotations in the air before landing back on the ramp. He has also invented many skateboarding tricks, including the McHawk, the Madonna, and the Stalefish. Although Hawk is retired from professional skateboarding, he is still active in several businesses, including video game consulting, film production, and clothing design.

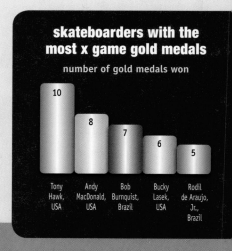

skateboarders with the most x game gold medals

number of gold medals won

10	8	7	6	5
Tony Hawk, USA	Andy MacDonald, USA	Bob Burnquist, Brazil	Bucky Lasek, USA	Rodil de Araujo, Jr., Brazil

athlete with the most x game medals

Dave Mirra

Dave Mirra has won 24 medals—14 gold, 6 silver, and 4 bronze—in X Game competition. He medaled in every X Game he entered between 1995 and 2005. All but three of Mirra's medals have come in BMX competition, in which he performs tricks such as double backflips, front flips, and triple tail whips. His last three medals were earned in rally car racing. In 2006, Mirra formed his own bike company named Mirraco, and he now competes for the company with other top BMX riders.

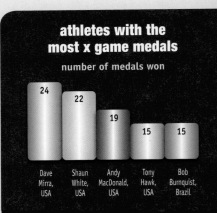

athletes with the most x game medals
number of medals won

Dave Mirra, USA	Shaun White, USA	Andy MacDonald, USA	Tony Hawk, USA	Bob Burnquist, Brazil
24	22	19	15	15

INDEX

PHOTO CREDITS

SCIENCE & TECHNOLOGY:
4–7 background: Marina Strizhak/iStockphoto; bubble: avean/iStockphoto; 4cl: rchagin/Shutterstock; br: ALiJA/iStockphoto; 5: Piti Tan/Shutterstock; 6tr: hackerkuper/Shutterstock; 6–7: Oleksiy Mark/Shutterstock; 7t: bannosuke/Shutterstock; cr: YellowPixel/Shutterstock; inset: bbirdy/iStockphoto; 8: Emily Teresa; 9: Mira/Alamy; 10: Handout/MCT/Newscom; 11: Eric Carr/Alamy; 12–13: Alex Segr/Alamy; 14: Tripplaar Kristoffer/SIPA/Newscom; 15: NetPhotos/Alamy; 16: Richard Levine/Alamy; 17: razorpi/Alamy; 18: Rune Hellestad/Corbis; 19: Vika Sabo/Alamy; 20: incamerastock/Alamy; 21: Charles Krupa/AP Images; 22: Mary Evans/STUDIO GHIBLI/Ronald Grant/Everett Collection; 23: Richard Levin/Alamy; 24: Blend Images/Shutterstock; 25: Zhudifeng/Dreamstime; 26: Bloomberg via Getty Images; 27: Davide Illini/iStockphoto; 28tl: Nir Alon/Alamy; tr: Andres Rodriguez/Alamy; 29: Ian Dagnall/Alamy; 30: Greenland/Dreamstime; 31: Laszlo Halasi/Shutterstock; 32: AFP/Getty Images; 33: BIGFOOT 4x4, Inc, 2011; 34: Shelley Mays/AP Photo; 35: Getty Images; 36: Ahmad Faizal Yahya/Dreamstime; 37: Fabrice Coffrini/AFP/Getty Images/Newscom; 38: C. David LaBianca/Sikokorsky; 39: Danjaq/Eon/UA/The Kobal Collection; 40: NASA; 41: Mike Derer/AP Photo; 42: Travis Schaeffer/Dreamstime; 43, 44: Ferrari World, Abu Dhabi; 45: Kamran Jebreili/AP Photo; 46: Focus/Alamy; 47: Korean Central News Agency via Korea News Service/AP Photo; 48: Barry Williams/Getty Images; 49: Imaginechina/AP Photo; 50: Galina Barskaya/People Dreamstime; 51: Steve Allen/Getty Images.

MONEY:
52–55 background: Marina Strizhak/iStockphoto; bubble: avean/iStockphoto; 52: John Angelillo/Newscom; 53: Kyodo/AP Photo; 54t: Bob Donnan/US PRESSWIRE; b: Jon Naustdalslid/Shutterstock; 55t: PRM/SIPA/Newscom; b: National News/Newscom; 56: President Wilson Hotel, Geneva; 57: Timothy A. Clary/AFP/Getty Images; 58: Bas Czerwinski/AP Photo; 59: Laurent Cipriani/AP Photo; 60: Fabrice Coffrini/Gatty Images; 61: Cal Sport Media/APPhoto; 62: Ronald Martinez/Getty Images; 63: Justin Aller/Getty Images; 64: Harifulin Valery/ITAR-TASS/Landov; 65: Icon SMI AAB/Icon SMI/Newscom; 66: Brian Kimball/KimballStock; 67: Bruce Glassman; 68: Robert Convery/Alamy; 69: Dale de la Rey/Bloomberg via Getty Images.

POP CULTURE:
70–73 background: Marina Strizhak/iStockphoto; bubble: avean/iStockphoto; 70: Lionsgate/Courtesy Everett Collection; 71: Adrian Sanchez-Gonzalez/CBS/Landov; 72t: Rex Features via AP Photo; b: Nick White/Media Bakery; 73: MCT/Getty Images; 74: HO/Reuters/Landov; 75: Barry King/Getty Images; 76: Charles Sykes/AP Photo; 77: Craig Barritt/WireImage/Getty Images; 78: Reed Saxon/AP Photo; 79: Jason Merritt/Getty Images; 80: CBS via Getty Images; 81: Jason Squires/Getty Images; 82: Cliff Lipson/CBS/Landov; 83: Mark J. Terrill/AP Photo; 84: Evan Agostini/AP Photo; 85: Kevork Djansezian/AP Photo; 86: Matt Sayles/AP Photo; 87: Jason Merritt/Getty Images; 88: Matt Sayles/AP Photo; 89: Universal Pictures/Photofest; 90: ZUMA Press/Newscom; 91: Richie Buxo/Splash News/Newscom; 92: Twentieth Century Fox Film Corporation/Photofest; 93: Nick Ut/AP Photo; 94: ZUMA Press/Newscom; 95: Serge Haouzi-Patrice Lapoirie/Maxppp/Landov; 96: 90/g90/ZUMA Press/Newscom; 97: Stephen Vaughan/Buena Vista Pictures/Photofest; 98, 99: Courtesy Everett Collection; 100: Ben Glass/Warner Bros/Regency/Canal+/The Kobal Collection; 101: AP Photo; 102–103: Leon Neal/Getty Images; 104: CFI/Splash News/Newscom; 105: Jon Kopaloff/Getty Images; 106: Bill Frakes/Getty Images; 107: Chris Pizzello/AP Photo; 108–109: Malte Christians/Zuma Press; 110: Esteban Dato/Zuma Press; 111: Jemal Countess/Getty Images; 112: Dan MacMedan/Getty Images; 113: Evan Agostin/AP Photo; 114: DPA/Zuma Press; 115: Mark Humphrey/AP Photo; 116: David Karp/AP Photo; 117: Greg Wood/AFP/Getty Images.

NATURE:
118–121 background: Marina Strizhak/iStockphoto; bubble: avean/iStockphoto; 118: James H. Robinson/Photo Researchers, Inc.; 119: Bill Curtsinger/National Geographic Stock; 120: valdezrl/Fotolia; 121t: Courtesy Gaetan Borgonie/Ghent University; b: Marc Szeglat/Photo Researchers, Inc.; 122: Borsheim's Jewelry Store/AP Photo; 123: Pichugin Dmitry/Shutterstock; 124: Eye Ubiquitous/Alamy; 125: Galyna Andrushko/Shutterstock; 126: Baloncici/Dreamstime; 127: Vladislav Turchenko/Dreamstime; 128: jele/Shutterstock; 129: ESRI/AP Photo; 130: Lacz, Gerard/Animals Animals; 131: Tasmania Parks and Wildlife Service, HO/AP Photo; 132: Photomyeye/Dreamstime; 133: Media Bakery; 134:

Tony Ludovico/AP Photo; 135: Tom Brakefield/Media Bakery; 136: Visuals Unlimited/Corbis; 137: Jens Kuhfs/Getty Images; 138: Gail Johnson/Dreamstime; 139: Jan Martin Will/Shutterstock; 140: Peter Johnson/Corbis; 141: Brian Grant/Dreamstime; 142: Keith Begg/Corbis; 143: Yva Momatiuk & John Eastcott/Minden Pictures; 144: FloridaStock/Shutterstock; 145: Oleg Znamenskiy/Dreamstime; 146: Ryszard Laskowski/Dreamstime; 147: Kelly Funk/Getty Images; 148: Roughcollie/Dreamstime; 149: Sylvain Cordier/Biosphoto; 150: Javarman/Dreamstime; 151: Gerrit De Vries/Dreamstime; 152: Frank Krahmer/Masterfile; 153: Dr. P. Marazzi/Photo Researchers, Inc.; 154: David A. Northcott/Corbis; 155, 156, 157: Joe McDonald/Corbis; 158: HO/REUTERS/Newscom; 159: Andrew Murray/Nature Picture Library; 160: Driverjcs/Dreamstime; 161: Franco Banfi/Getty Images; 162: Pete Oxford/Minden; 163: Dave Massey/Dreamstime; 164: Ted Levin/Animals Animals; 165: Deborah Hewitt/Dreamstime; 166: Dompr/Dreamstime; 167: Nagel Photography/Shutterstock; 168: Linn Currie/Shutterstock; 169: Dean Pennala/Shutterstock; 170: Staffan Widstrand/Corbis; 171: Media Bakery; 172: Juan Manuel Barreto/AP Photo; 173: David Garry/Dreamstime; 174: Suzanne Long/Alamy; 175: Beisea/Dreamstime; 176: William Perry/Dreamstime; 177: George McCarthy/Corbis; 178: Kira Kaplinski/Dreamstime; 179: Lloyd Cluff/Corbis; 180: Corbis; 181: Phil Coale/AP Photo; 182: Roberto Borea/AP Photo; 183: Bill Greenblatt/UPI/Landov; 184: Jack Thornell/AP Photo; 185: Davo Blair/Alamy.

US RECORDS:

186–189 background: Marina Strizhak/iStockphoto; bubble: avean/iStockphoto; 186: Revenant/Shutterstock; 187t: Hemera Technologies/Thinkstock; b: Win McNamee/Getty Images; 188t: Naturalight/Dreamstime; b: Steve Prorak/Dreamstime; 189: Springboard, Inc./iStockphoto; 190: William Manning/Corbis; 191: Mark A. Johnson/Corbis; 192: Ron Adcock/Dreamstime; 193: Belliot/Dreamstime; 194: Jed Jacobsohn/Getty Images; 195: Tony Sweet/MediaBakery; 196: Courtesy Lake Compounce; 197: Luc Viatour/Wikipedia; 198: Jeff Kinsey/Dreamstime; 199: Georgia Sports Hall of Fame; 200: Roger Ressmeyer/Corbis; 201: Courtesy of www.sodaspringsid.com; 202: SongquanDeng/Shutterstock; 203: Ed Bock/Corbis; 204: Kim Pin Tan/Dreamstime; 205: Scott T. Smith/Corbis; 206: AP Photo; 207: Ocean/Corbis; 208: Layne Kennedy/Corbis; 210: Kevin Fleming/Corbis; 211: Andrew Horne/Wikipedia; 212: Bill Ross/Corbis; 213: Philip Gould/Corbis; 214: James A. Finley/AP Photo; 215: Sekernas/Dreamstime; 216: Bill Grant/Alamy; 217: David Samuel Robbins/Corbis; 218: Zentilia/Shutterstock; 219: Bob Krist/Corbis; 220: Steve Estvanik/Shutterstock; 221: John Munson/Star Ledger/Corbis; 222: Monkey Business Images/Dreamstime;

223: Gary Greff; 224: Evan Hurd/Corbis; 225: John Elk III/Getty Images; 226: Bruce Shippee/Dreamstime; 227: Darlene Bordwell; 228: Bob Krist/Corbis; 229: Yalonda M. James/Post and Courier/AP Photo; 230: Tom Bean/Corbis; 231: Courtesy the Tennessee Aquarium; 232: Richard Cummins/Corbis; 233: Leon7/Wikipedia; 234: Anikasalsera/Dreamstime; 235: Don S. Montgomery/Corbis; 236: George White Location Photography; 237: Jacek Jasinski/Shutterstock; 238: Amy Muller/Noah's Ark; 239: Michael Smith/The Wyoming Tribune Eagle/AP Photo.

SPORTS:

240–243 background: Marina Strizhak/iStockphoto; bubble: avean/iStockphoto; 240tl: LOCOG/AP Photo; b: Jgade/Shutterstock; 241t: Ben Pruchnie/Getty Images for McDonald's; 242: Ed Reinke/AP Photo; 243t: Anthony Devlin/AP Photo; b: Don Tran/Shutterstock; 244: Jim Bourg/Reuters/Corbis; 245: Beth A. Keiser/AP Photo; 246: Bettmann/Corbis; 247: Alan Diaz/AP Photo; 248: US Presswire; 249: Richard Mackson/Sports Illustrated/Getty Images; 250: Bill Baptist/WNBAE via Getty Images; 251: Walker/UTHM/Icon SMI/Newscom; Andrew D. Bernstein/NBAE via Getty Images; 253: Jim Rogash/Getty Images; 254: Ed Zurga/AP Photo; 255: Philip James Corwin/Corbis; 256: Jeffrey Phelps/AP Photo; 257: Marc Serota/Reuters/Corbis; 258: Greg Fiume/Corbis; 259: Denis Poroy/AP Photo; 260: Al Behrman/AP Photo; 261: Kevin Rivoli/AP Photo; 262: Hans Deryk/AP Photo; 263: Justin Edmonds/Getty Images; 264: Mary Schwalm/AP Photo; 265: Mark Humphrey/AP Photo; 266: Oliver Hoslet/epa/Corbis; 267: Lou Novick/Cal Sport Media/Newscom; 268: Chris Trotman/Getty Images; 269: Alan Diaz/AP Photo; 270: Duomo/Corbis; 271: Reuters/Corbis; 272: Elise Amendola/AP Photo; 273: Denis Poroy/AP Photo; 274: Ron Heflin/AP Photo; 275: Wally McNamee/Corbis; 276: Bettmann/Corbis; 277: MLB Photos via Getty Images; 278: Harry Harris/AP Photo; 279: Reuters/Corbis; 280: John O'Boyle/Corbis; 281: Gregg Newton/Corbis; 282: Bettmann/Corbis; 283: Bettmann/Corbis; 284: Roberto Borea/AP Photo; 285: Francois Lenoir/Reuters/Corbis; 286: Rick Stevens/AP Photo; 287: Alan Diaz/AP Photo; 288: Mike Lawn/Fox Photos/Getty Images; 289: Mike Hewitt/Getty Images; 290: Jayne Kamin-Oncea/US PRESSWIRE; 291: Kevork Djansezian/AP Photo; 292: Ben Curtis/AP Photo; 293: Jean-Yves Ruszniewski/TempSport/Corbis; 294: Fritz Reiss/AP Photo; 295: AP Photo; 296: Reinhold Matay/AP Photo; 297: Jim Cole/AP Photo; 298: Jerome Miron/US PRESSWIRE; 299: Mirco Lazzari gp/Getty Images; 300: Gert Eggenberger/AP Photo; 301: Jim Wells/AP Photo; 302: David E. Klutho/Sports Illustrated/Getty Images; 303: Bettmann/Corbis; 304: Bill Kostroun/AP Photo; 305: Ryan Remiorz/AP Photos; 306: Rick Rickman/NewSport/Corbis; 307: Duomo/Corbis.

Read for the World Record!

KIDS ANSWERED THE CHALLENGE!

Kids from every state and around the world participated in the Scholastic Summer Challenge to set a record for summer reading!

As part of the Summer Challenge, Read for the World Record united students in an attempt to achieve a world record by reading as many minutes as possible between May 1 and August 31, 2012.

CONGRATULATIONS TO ALL STUDENTS WHO HELPED SET THE RECORD!

Total minutes read from
May 1 to August 31, 2012: **95,859,491**

Millions of Reading Minutes

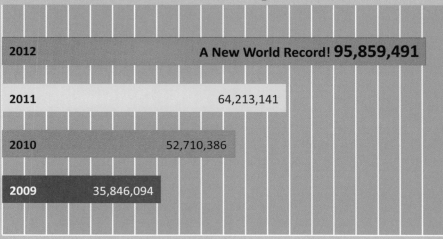

2012	A New World Record! 95,859,491
2011	64,213,141
2010	52,710,386
2009	35,846,094

0 5 10 15 20 25 30 35 40 45 50 55 60 65 70 75 80 85 90 95 100

Read for the World Record!

CHECK OUT THESE COOL FACTS:

TOP 20 STATES WITH THE MOST MINUTES READ:

1. Texas
2. Florida
3. North Carolina
4. Illinois
5. New York
6. Pennsylvania
7. New Jersey
8. Georgia
9. Alabama
10. California
11. Massachusetts
12. Colorado
13. Ohio
14. Michigan
15. Virginia
16. South Carolina
17. Wisconsin
18. Minnesota
19. Missouri
20. Utah

STATES WITH THE MOST MINUTES READ

Did your state make the top 20?

BIG STATE, BIG IMPROVEMENT!

Texas led the nation in minutes read this summer with 16,054,221. That's nearly five times the minutes they entered last year, and the Aldine School District in Houston had three schools in the top 20.

STUDENTS FROM AROUND THE WORLD PARTICIPATED!

Three international schools read enough minutes to rank in the top 100 worldwide: Seoul Foreign School in Seoul, South Korea (#27); Our Lady of Mercy School in Rio de Janeiro, Brazil (#41); and Newry High School in Newry, Northern Ireland (#77). Schools from 32 countries contributed minutes to the new world record, including:

Canada
China
Colombia

Cyprus
Dubai
Egypt

Netherlands
Nicaragua
South Korea

Thailand
United Kingdom
U.S. Virgin Islands

Total number of participating schools:

4,446

Total number of students:

193,621

Members of Brooksville Elementary School
with their minutes.

SMALL TOWN, BIG IMPACT!

Top honor in the 2012 Scholastic Summer Challenge goes to **Brooksville Elementary School** in Brooksville, FL, with **3,463,452** minutes logged toward the new summer reading world record. The population in the town of Brooksville is just 7,264 people, yet elementary school students read a combined 6,639,861 minutes in the summers of 2011 and 2012!

THE TOP 20 SUMMER READING SCHOOLS!

The following schools are recognized for their outstanding contributions toward setting a new world record:

Brooksville Elementary School	Brooksville, FL	3,463,452
Sun Valley Elementary School	Monroe, NC	2,567,912
Paine Intermediate School	Trussville, AL	1,816,380
Hill Intermediate School	Houston, TX	1,290,609
St. Gregory Elementary School	Tyler, TX	1,230,063
Savannah Country Day School	Savannah, GA	1,165,200
Village Elementary School	Hilton, NY	1,092,331
Oakridge Middle School	Clover, SC	1,072,746
Worsham Elementary School	Houston, TX	1,057,259
Odom Elementary School	Houston, TX	1,015,633
Valley Intermediate School	Pelham, AL	1,009,897
Bright Horizons	Charlotte, NC	999,643
George L. Hess Educational Complex	Mays Landing, NJ	907,524
Riverview Elementary School	Saratoga Springs, UT	884,329
IDEA Frontier Academy	Brownsville, TX	873,380
Liberty Park Elementary School	Greenacres, FL	849,183
Newell Elementary School	Allentown, NJ	844,801
Scott Elementary School	Melrose Park, IL	832,471
Enders-Salk Elementary School	Schaumburg, IL	828,446
Reedy Creek Elementary School	Kissimmee, FL	824,425

Read for the World Record!

THE BEST OF THE REST!

These schools all logged more than 500,000 minutes toward setting the new world record!

School	Location	Minutes
Parsons Elementary School	Suwanee, GA	812,599
Carmichael Elementary School	Houston, TX	777,591
Sabal Palm Elementary School	Naples, FL	775,313
Gettysburg Area Middle School	Gettysburg, PA	721,257
Ballantyne Elementary School	Charlotte, NC	653,288
Emmet D. Williams Elementary School	Shoreview, MN	644,162
Coral Reef Elementary School	Lake Worth, FL	605,172
Highland Elementary School	Sylvania, OH	604,668
Bowie Memorial School	Chicopee, MA	573,993
Dovalina Elementary School	Laredo, TX	549,032
Fairview Elementary School	Hoffman Estates, IL	536,304
Jim Thorpe Area School District	Jim Thorpe, PA	527,973
Stehlik Intermediate School	Houston, TX	525,597
Imagine School	St. Petersburg, FL	523,986
Holy Family Catholic Academy	Honolulu, HI	523,207
Stephens Elementary School	Houston, TX	521,791

187 schools logged **100,000** minutes or more!

SCHOLASTIC
SUMMER CHALLENGE

WWW.SCHOLASTIC.COM/SUMMER